IN YOUR POCKET

A handy directory of restaurants, hotels, museums, theaters, stores, nightlife, famous landmarks—the best of the city's sights, services, and pleasures!

Fourth Edition

BARRON'S

New York • London • Toronto • Sydney

Credits

Maps of Rapid Transit Lines and Commuter Rail Lines reprinted courtesy of Massachusetts Bay Transportation Authority.

Book design by Milton Glaser, Inc.
Illustrations by Marc Rosenthal

Inclusion of a particular store or service in this guide should not be construed as a recommendation from the Publisher. All noted sources and services subject to change; we suggest that you phone ahead.

All inquiries should be addressed to:
Barron's Educational Series, Inc.
250 Wireless Boulevard
Hauppauge, New York 11788

Library of Congress Catalog Card No. 86-22285

International Standard Book No.
0-8120-3767-7

Library of Congress Cataloging in Publication Data
Boston in your pocket.

   Bibliography: p.19
   1. Boston (Mass.)–Description–1981– –Guidebooks. I. Barron's Educational Series, Inc.
F73.18.B664   1987   917.44′610443   86-22285
ISBN 0-8120-3767-7

PRINTED IN THE UNITED STATES OF AMERICA

789   969   98765432

CONTENTS

Contents

Contents

PREFACE

Puritans and Patriots, Minute Men and Sons of Liberty. A famous Tea Party and Paul Revere's midnight ride. Harvard, MIT, and a score of colleges and universities. The restrained elegance of neighborhoods like Beacon Hill and Back Bay. Adams, Longfellow, Kennedy. Just the names of the streets in Boston and Cambridge would tell most of America's history. The Puritans settled here in the 1630s; the Revolution began here in the mid-1770s; less than a century later Boston was the cultural capital of the nation and the unofficial arbiter of its taste and mores. Today the largest city in New England continues its important and exciting history. One look at the downtown area between Beacon Hill and the harbor shows the kind of vitality that characterizes the city. The waterfront area has been thoroughly renovated and is again one of the city's commercial focal points with the Faneuil Hall Market Place area and the housing on Long Wharf and Lewis Wharf. New buildings are going up in the Government Center area; one of the most striking additions several years ago was Boston's new City Hall, an architectural achievement in its own right. And this area, located on the site of the original Puritan settlement, is linked with Boston's other historical attractions in the North End, on Beacon Hill, and across the Charles River at Bunker Hill in Charlestown by the Freedom Trail.

But there is more to Boston than its downtown and harbor areas. Beyond the Common and just the other side of the Public Garden there are Back Bay's lively commercial stretches (Boylston Street to the Prudential Center), the seemingly endless art galleries and boutiques of Newbury Street, the opulent new shopping galleries, restaurants, and hotels of Copley Place (on the south side of Copley Square, across from Boston Public Library), and the row upon row of quiet, comfortable brick residences that characterize the neighborhood. Across the Charles River, Cambridge, a city in its own right, is blossoming with smart shops, popular night spots, and important additions to the universities there.

What characterizes the Boston area? It is perhaps, this very combination of the old and the new—sometimes discordant, but somehow blended by a combination of civic concern and pride, a sense of urban aesthetic, and a recognition that Boston is not just another American city. Walk the Freedom Trail. Along the route you see this: brick house or church, circa 1750; glass and steel or concrete office tower, circa 1980—and it all fits.

Acknowledgments

We gratefully acknowledge the help of Andrew Rubenfeld in researching and preparing the material for the first edition. We are thankful to Christopher Billy, who researched and revised the book for its second edition. We also thank Robert Cutler and Andy Gaus for their help with the third edition. We further thank Leslie Wheeler, who revised the book for its fourth edition.

A HOME IN BEACON HILL

THE CITY, SUBURBS, AND STATE

Officially the Commonwealth of Massachusetts, the state is also known by its 2 nicknames: the Bay State and the Old Colony State. Massachusetts itself comes from 2 Indian words meaning "great mountain place." As a colonial entity, present-day Massachusetts was originally Plymouth Colony (founded by the Pilgrims in 1620) and Massachusetts Bay Colony (founded by the Puritans in 1630); they were combined well before the Revolution. Massachusetts entered the Union in 1788 as the sixth state. Its motto, translated from the Latin, is "By the sword we seek peace, but peace only under liberty." The state flower is the mayflower; the state bird the chickadee. In terms of population, Massachusetts ranks eleventh with over 5.7 million inhabitants (1980 census); in terms of land area (7,826 square miles) the state is the forty-fifth. There are 14 counties. The largest cities (1980 census) are Boston (562,994), Worcester (161,799), and Springfield (152,319).

Boston, the state capital, occupies 46 square miles in Suffolk County, at the mouths of the Charles and Mystic rivers on Massachusetts Bay. Its geographic situation gives it and the surrounding metropolitan area the nickname of "The Hub of New England." Greater Boston has a population of over 2.7 million people (1980 census). It includes the city of Boston, the city of Cambridge (across the Charles River from Boston), and suburban towns and communities such as Quincy, Weymouth, Braintree, and Milton to the south; Brookline, Newton, Needham, Natick, Wellesley, and Framingham to the west; and Watertown, Waltham, Somerville, Arlington, Lexington, Concord, Medford, Woburn, Chelsea, Everett, Revere, Lynn, and Salem to the north. Boston was founded in 1630 by the Puritans on a marshy area of the Shawmut Peninsula and was named after the city of Boston in England. The name "Boston" is a shortening of "St. Botolph's town," after its original English patron saint.

ACCOMMODATIONS

See HOTELS, MOTELS, BED AND BREAKFAST.

AFTERNOON TEA

See COFFEE and TEA.

ANNUAL EVENTS

All information courtesy of the Greater Boston Convention & Visitors Bureau. For details, check the local papers' calendar sections, especially the "Calendar" section of Thursday's *Boston Globe* and the listings in the "Arts" section of the *Boston Phoenix*.

January

First Night, New Year's Eve—entertainment in various parts of the city; call 424-1699.
New England Camping and Recreational Vehicle Show, Bayside Exposition Center; call 242-6092.

February

New England Boat Show, Bayside Exposition Center; call 242-6092.
Black History Month—check newspaper and magazine listings for special programs.
Ice Follies, Boston Garden; call 227-3206.
Chinese New Year, Beach and Tyler Streets; call 542-2574.
Beanpot Tournament—college hockey at the Boston Garden; call 227-3200.
North American Home Show, Bayside Exposition Center; call 242-6092.
Motorcycle and ATV Expo, Bayside Exposition Center; call 250-8060.

March

Boston Globe Jazz and Heritage Festival, Opera House, Berklee Performance Center, and other locations; call 929-2649.

Boston Gift Show, Bayside Exposition Center; call 686-6070.

New England Spring Flower Show, Bayside Exposition Center; call 536-9280.

St. Patrick's Day Celebration, South Boston; call 268-8525.

Great Egg Race, Museum of Science; call 723-2500.

Maple Sugaring Demonstrations, Blue Hills Trailside Museum.

Evacuation Day Parade, South Boston, Sunday before St. Patrick's Day (March 17th).

Avon Tennis Championship Finals, Walter Brown Arena, Boston University.

U.S.S. Constitution Model Shipwrights Guild Show, U.S.S. *Constitution* Museum.

Shamrock Classic, Causeway Street.

East Coast Athletic Conference Hockey Championships, Boston Garden.

Easter Parade (March or April), Commonwealth Avenue to the Public Garden.

April

Massachusetts Special Olympics; call 451-5747.

Boston Marathon, Hopkinton Common to Copley Square; call 435-6905.

WBCN Rock 'N' Roll Expo, Bayside Exposition Center; call 266-1111.

Yale Whiffenpoof vs. Harvard Crocodillo Concert, Stone Zoo.

March to Concord, Minute Man National Historical Park.

Spring Town Meeting, Old Sturbridge Village.

Puppet Week, Children's Museum.

Prince Hall Grand Chapter of Royal Arch Masons Parade, Franklin Field.

Walk America Walkathon March of Dimes, City Hall Plaza.

Red Sox Season Opener, Fenway Park; call 267-8661.

Artists' Ball, Boston Center for the Arts–Cyclorama; call 227-2443.

Azalea Festival, Faneuil Hall; call 523-2980.

Swan Boats Opening Day, Public Gardens.

Patriots' Day Weekend Celebrations; call 536-4100.

May

Beacon Hill Annual Hidden Gardens Tour, Beacon Hill.

Annual Cambridge River Festival, Cambridge Common.

Truck Show, Bayside Exposition Center; call 242-6092.

May Day Celebration Song & Dance, Blue Hills Trailside Museum.

New England Film Festival, New England Life Hall, Boston Film Video Foundation; call 536-1540.

Art Newbury Street, Newbury Street between Arlington Street and Massachusetts Avenue; call 267-9416.

Lilac Sunday, Arnold Arboretum; call 524-1718.

New England Street Performers Festival, Faneuil Hall; call 523-2980.

Kite Festival, Franklin Park Zoo.

Official Opening of Franklin Park Zoo.

The Revels, Sanders Theater, Cambridge; call 426-0889.

West End House Road Race, 105 Allston Street.

June

Ancient & Honorable Artillery Company Parade, Faneuil Hall to the State House; call 277-1638.

Cambridge River Festival, Memorial Drive on the Charles River; call 498-9033.

Boston Common Dairy Festival, Boston Common; call 523-2110.

Bunker Hill Day Parade, Charlestown; call 241-9511.

Hammond Castle Annual Medieval Festival, Gloucester; call 283-7673.

Blessing of the Fleets, Provincetown and Gloucester.

St. Botolph Street Fair, St. Botolph Street.

Dorchester Day Parade, Dorchester; call 725-4000.
Scooper Bowl, Boston Common.
Victorian Promenade at the Public Garden.
Back Bay Street Fair, Marlborough Street.
Blue Hills Farm Days, Blue Hills Trailside Museum.
Festival of the Future, DeCordova Museum.
Art & Antiques in the Park, Boston Common.
St. Anthony Festival, Prince Street.

July

Annual Turnaround Cruise of U.S.S. Constitution, Boston Harbor.
Harbor Walk, Boston Tea Party Ship and Museum.
4th of July Parade, Minute Man National Historical Park.
Harborfest, July 4th celebration on the waterfront; call 536-4100.
4th of July Fireworks and free Boston Pops Concert, The Esplanade; call 266-1492.
Haying Contest, Old Sturbridge Village.
Marblehead Arts Festival; call 631-2868.
Madonna della Grazia Italian Festival, Endicott Street.
St. Rocco Italian Festival, North Margin Street.
Union Warren Bank U.S. Pro Tennis Championships, Longwood Tennis Club; call 731-2900 or 731-4500.
Bastille Day, Marlboro Street; call 266-4351.
Ladies Professional Golf Association Tournament, Sheraton Tara Hotel and Resort at Ferncroft, Danvers; call 523-2281.
Puerto Rican Day Festival; call 725-4395.
Independence Day Oration and Parade, Faneuil Hall.
Harborfest Fireworks Concert, Charlestown Navy Yard; call 227-1528 or 876-7777.
Bay State Games; call 727-3227.
Boston Seafood Festival, Boston Fish Pier; call 727-4107.

August

Sandcastle Competition, Crane's Beach.
Fishermen's Festival, North Street.

Annual Events

6

St. Anthony, St. Lucy, and St. Rosalie Italian Festivals, North End.
Kidsfair, Boston Common, WBZ-TV; call 787-7000.
August Moon Festival, Chinatown.

September

Governor's Cup Race, Boston Common; call 267-0055.
Charles Street Fair, Beacon Hill Civic Association.
International Sailboat Show, Newport.
Art Newbury Street; call 267-9416.
New England Apple Fair, Faneuil Hall; call 523-2980.
Greek Heritage Festival, Waterfront Park.
Footlight Parade, Park Plaza Hotel.
Lowell Regatta, Lowell.
Annual Cranberry Festival, Edaville Railroad.

October

Tufts 10-K Race for Women; call 267-0055.
Globe Book Fair, Boston Sheraton Hotel.
Octoberfest Street Fair, Harvard Square.
Honey Harvest, Blue Hills Trailside Museum.
Apple Days, Blue Hills Trailside Museum.
Columbus Day Parade, East Boston to North End; call 725-4000.
Head of the Charles Regatta, Charles River; call 227-2815 or 868-0194.
Annual Bourne Bay Scallop Festival, Buzzard's Bay.
Harvest Celebration, Plymouth Plantation.
Boston Freedom Trail Road Race; call 846-6682.
Halloween Costume Ball, Hammond Castle Museum, Gloucester; call 283-2080.
Monsterdash, Halloween fun run; call 523-2980.

November

Thanksgiving Celebration, Old Sturbridge Village.
Veteran's Day Parade, Back Bay.
Thanksgiving Day Road Race, Downtown Crossing; call 267-0055.
Christmas Festival, Edaville Railroad.
Purity Supreme Heartbreak Hill Road Race; call 267-0055.

Harvard-Yale Football Game, Harvard Stadium (even-numbered years).
New England International Auto Show, Bayside Exposition Center; call 536-8156.
Eastern Dog Shows, Bayside Exposition Center; call 726-2924.
Ski Show, Bayside Exposition Center; call 242-6582.

December

Reenactment of Boston Tea Party, Boston Tea Party Ship.
Pops New Year's Eve Concert, Symphony Hall.
Christmas Eve Caroling, Louisburg Square, Beacon Hill.
Marblehead Christmas Walk; call 631-2868.
Candlelight and Caroling Service, Trinity Church.
The Revels, Sanders Theater, Cambridge; call 739-7940.
Handel and Hayden Society's Messiah, Symphony Hall; call 266-1492.
Christmas Star Show, Science Museum; call 723-2505.
The Nutcracker Suite, Boston Ballet, Wang Center; call 542-1323.
Christmas Antiques and Crafts Show, Bayside Exposition Center; call 462-7096.

ANTIQUES

Charles Street, in Beacon Hill, has a good selection of antique shops, some traditional and expensive and some with surprising finds and bargains. There are also a number of shops in Back Bay, especially on Newbury Street. Antique shops dot the countryside around Boston. Generally the farther you are from Boston or a popular town, the more likely you are to find a good deal. Keep an eye out for garage sales, flea markets, and auctions. Southern New Hampshire, central Massachusetts, and northern Rhode Island are good areas to check. Some establishments in Boston are listed below:

A. C. Kim Oriental Antiques 134 Charles Street (367-1200). Good for porcelain.

Allen Gilbert and Company 11 Beacon Street (523-4220). Books, prints, coins, and stamps, plus antique American clocks and watches. By appointment only.

Appleton Antiques 544 Tremont Street (482-4910). Victorian furniture and accessories.

Bay Colony Antiques 96 Charles Street (227-9097). General selection.

Bedlam Brass Beds 167 Massachusetts Avenue, Arlington (696-8698). Brass beds and brass accessories.

Bernheimer's Antique Arts 52C Brattle Street, Cambridge (547-1177). European, Asian, and primitive.

Blue Moon 306 Newbury Street (262-7575). Eclectic paintings, furniture, jewelry.

Brodney Gallery of Fine Arts 811 Boylston Street (536-0500). Paintings, bronzes, and jewelry.

Charles Street Trading Post 99 Charles Street (367-9551). Collectibles, furniture.

City Lights 2226 Massachusetts Avenue, Cambridge (547-1490). Antique lighting, 1880–1930.

Country Fair Antique & Flea Market Salem Street (Rte. 129) in Reading (944-7882). Take exit 34 off Rte. 128. 200 dealers man their booths every Sunday from 9 to 5.

Forever Flamingo 285 Newbury Street (267-2547). Art Deco porcelain as well as vintage clothing and jewelry.

George Gravert 122 Charles Street (227-1593). French country furniture.

Holly Hill Antiques 48 Weston Street (Rte. 20) in Waltham (891-0300). Take exit 49 off Rte. 128. One of the largest collections in the Northeast.

Hurst & Hurst 53 Mount Auburn Street, Cambridge (491-6888). Oriental and primitive art.

Hyman Grossman 51 Charles Street (523-1879). American furniture.

James Moriarty 115 Charles Street (227-6113). 17th-, 18th-, and 19th-century French and Italian furniture.

Marcoz Antiques 177 Newbury Street (262-0780). Unusual furniture, decorative accessories, and jewelry.

Marika's Antique Shop 130 Charles Street (523-4520). European and American.

Music Emporium, Inc. 2018 Massachusetts Avenue, Cambridge (661-2099). Antique musical instruments.

Phoebe 214 Newbury Street (262-4148). General selection.

Pleasant Galleries 58 Pleasant Street, Dorchester (265-4212). Furniture, Oriental rugs, clocks, and bric-a-brac. Auctions and appraisals.

Samuel L. Lowe, Jr. Antiques 80 Charles Street (742-0845). Marine antiques.

Shells of England, Ltd. 84 Chestnut Street (523-0373). English and American Antiques.

Shreve, Crump and Low 330 Boylston Street (267-9100). Fine English and American objects.

Simpson Jewelers 50 Bromfield Street (542-1680).

Sotheby's 101 Newbury Street (247-2851). Fine art and jewelry. By appointment only.

Weiner's Antique Shop 22 Beacon Street, opposite the State House (227-2894). Appraisals and estimates in addition to retail trade.

AQUARIUMS

The **New England Aquarium** is located on Central Wharf, a few blocks directly east of the Faneuil Hall-Quincy Market area. The nearest subway station is Aquarium on the Blue Line. The aquarium has over 7,000 fresh and saltwater fish on display as well as sea turtles, otters, harbor seals, dolphins, sea lions, electric eels, penguins, and octopuses. Hours are Monday–Thursday 9 A.M.–5 P.M., Fridays 9 A.M.–9 P.M. Saturdays, Sundays, and holidays 9 A.M.– 5 P.M. (longer hours during the summer). Admission for adults is $5.50, for children $3.25. For further information, write New England Aquarium, Central Wharf, Boston, Massachusetts 02110; or telephone 742-8870.

ART GALLERIES

Newbury Street has the greatest concentration of art galleries in Boston, if not in the country. Gallery hours vary, but virtually all are closed Sunday and Monday, and the most frequently found schedule is Tuesday through Saturday, 10 A.M.–5:30 P.M. Check the *Boston Phoenix's* "Arts Listings," in the Arts section, or pick up the *Boston/New England Gallery Guide* at any gallery.

Alianza Gallery 140 Newbury Street (262-2385). Contemporary American handicrafts, ceramics, art glass, jewelry, quilts.

Alpha Gallery 121 Newbury Street (536-4465). Contemporary painting.

Barbara Krakow Gallery 10 Newbury Street (262-4490). Contemporary painting and drawing.

Bromfield Gallery 36 Newbury Street (262-7782). Collectively owned gallery showing works by Boston-area artists.

Childs Gallery 169 Newbury Street (266-1108). Classic paintings, prints and drawings.

David Bernstein Gallery 36 Newbury Street (267-3779). Entirely devoted to artworks in glass.

Francesca Anderson Gallery 132 Newbury Street (262-1062). Specializing in contemporary realism.

Gallery 52 52 Charles Street (523-0204). Artist-owned collective.

Gallery Fofene 335A Newbury Street (437-0029). Glassware, sculpture, paintings, and jewelry by area artists.

Gallery in the Square 665 Boylston Street (426-6616). Modern graphics and painting.

Gallery NAGA 67 Newbury Street (267-9060). Contemporary regional painting and sculpture.

Gallery Nature and Temptation 40 Saint Stephen Street, behind Symphony Hall (247-1719). Paintings and ceramics in the Japanese tradition.

Goethe Institute 170 Beacon Street (262-6050). Periodic exhibits of works by German artists. The building itself has one of Boston's most beautiful interiors.

Harcus Gallery 7 Newbury Street (262-4445). Contemporary painting and drawing.

Iguana Gallery 246 Newbury Street (247-0211). Central and South American arts and crafts.

Kingston Gallery 129 Kingston Street (423-4113). Drawings, paintings, sculpture, installation, and performance art.

Laughlin/Winkler Gallery 205 A Street, Fort Point Channel, South Boston (269-1782). Collective gallery showing works in various media.

ISABELLA STEWART GARDNER MUSEUM

Lopoukhine Gallery 10 Newbury Street (262-4211). Contemporary painting, drawing, and sculpture.
Nielsen Gallery 179 Newbury Street (266-4835). Contemporary painting and sculpture.
Pucker Safrai Gallery 171 Newbury Street (267-9473). Contemporary paintings, sculpture, ceramics, prints.
Randall Beck Gallery 168 Newbury Street (262-4445). Contemporary painting and drawing.
Rolly-Michaux 290 Dartmouth Street (536-9898). Contemporary works in various media.
Signature 1 Dock Square, North Street (227-4885). Arts and crafts.
Society of Arts and Crafts 175 Newbury Street (266-1810). Various media including furniture.
Stavaridis Gallery 73 Newbury Street (353-1681). Contemporary works in various media.
Stux Gallery 36 Newbury Street (267-7300). Drawing and sculpture.
Vision Gallery of Photography 216 Newbury Street (266-9481). Contemporary photography.
Vose Gallery 238 Newbury Street (536-6176). The oldest gallery in America, specializing in 18th- and 19th-century American and European paintings.
Wenniger Graphics 174 Newbury Street (536-4688). Specializes in printmaking.
Westminster Gallery 132A Newbury Street (266-6704). Crafts, ceramics, and glass by Britain's best traditional craftsmen.

ART MUSEUMS

See MUSEUMS.

ART SUPPLIES

These shops are located all over the city. For basic stationery needs try the stores in the downtown area, especially near Government Center. For more artistic needs the shops near colleges with noted art departments or near the museums are good (the Museum of Fine Arts, for example, has its own art school).

Art at the Open Door 711 Boylston Street (267-3940). Students get 10 percent off with valid ID.

Bob Slate 1975 Massachusetts Avenue (547-8624), 30 Brattle Street (547-7181), and 1288 Massachusetts Avenue (547-1230). All in Cambridge. Good for paper, pens, and ink.

Bromfield Pen Shop 39 Bromfield Street (482-9053).

Charrette/Stones 45 Batterymarch Street (542-1666); 44 Brattle Street, Cambridge (495-0200); and 1033 Massachusetts Avenue, Cambridge (495-0235). Large selection for professional draftsmen and artists. Discount cards available.

Harvard Square Art Center 17 Holyoke Street, Cambridge (491-3883).

Johnson Artist Materials 355 Newbury Street (536-4065).

Lambert Company 920 Commonwealth Avenue (232-8551).

Massachusetts College of Arts Store 354 Brookline Avenue (566-3129) and 26 Overland Street (267-8664). Discount.

Sam Flax Art & Drafting 675 Massachusetts Avenue, Cambridge (354-8141).

Utrecht Art and Drafting Supplies 333 Massachusetts Avenue (262-4948).

BABYSITTERS

See CHILDREN AND CHILDREN'S THINGS.

BAKERIES AND PASTRY SHOPS

Cheesecake is one of the Boston area's specialties, as are the varieties of Italian pastries found in shops in the North End.

Au Bon Pain 52 Winter Street (338-8304); in Faneuil Hall Marketplace (742-8452); in the Prudential Cen-

Clothing

Filene's "Basement" In Filene's Department Store, 426 Washington Street (357-2324).

Hit or Miss 7 Massachusetts Avenue, Cambridge (491-9486) and other locations. Discount.

Loehmann's 594 Worcester Street, Natick (655-1750). Worth the trip for discounts on women's fashions.

Records

Harvard Coop 1400 Massachusetts Avenue in Cambridge (492-1000). Large selection and frequent sales.

Miscellaneous

Lechmere Sales 88 First Street, Cambridge (491-2000). Department store with many bargains.

Service Merchandise 264 Monsignor O'Brien Highway, Somerville (625-8750). Discount housewares, appliances.

Sherman's 11 Bromfield Street (482-9610). Appliances, housewares, etc.

BARS

See NIGHTLIFE.

BATHROOM ACCESSORIES

See HOUSEWARES AND KITCHENWARES.

BEACHES

See PARKS AND NATURE PRESERVES—SWIMMING.

BEAUTY SALONS

Eleganza Coiffure and Boutique 1638 Massachusetts Avenue (354-6878), and 52-D Brattle Street (876-4425). Both in Cambridge.
Hair Richard-Joseph, Inc. 164 Newbury Street (536-9678).
Ibis 119 Newbury Street (536-1811). Complete hair and skin services for men and women.
Louis of Boston 167 Tremont Street (542-6320). Hair salon for men, women, and children.
Louis Terramagra Salon Renaissance 71 Newbury Street (536-1700). Full-service salon.
Sasha Skin Care at Harvard Square Galeria Mall, 57 JFK Street, Cambridge (497-2210).

BED AND BREAKFAST

See HOTELS, MOTELS, BED AND BREAKFAST.

BOOKS AND BOOKSTORES

The Greater Boston Convention & Visitors Bureau issues two publications: the *Official Boston Map and Freedom Trail Guide* ($1) and the *Official Guide to Boston* ($2). These can be purchased at the bureau's information center at the beginning of the Freedom Trail—on the Tremont Street side of the Boston Common, near the Park Street MBTA Station—or at the Prudential Plaza Visitors Center. Information can be requested by mail:

Greater Boston Convention & Visitors Bureau
Visitor Services
P.O. Box 490
Boston, MA 02199

The National Park Service's **Boston National Historical Park** has a set of free brochures with excellent maps and texts. They can be obtained at the park's Visitor Information Center on the Freedom Trail between the Old State House and the Faneuil Hall-Quincy Market Area. There are also free brochures on other National Park Service units in the vicinity as well as a variety of historically oriented publications for sale.

Books and Maps

There is a trove of books and maps on Boston, many of which are carried in Boston's and Cambridge's numerous bookstores. One of the best and largest selections is found in the Globe Corner Bookstore at the corner of School and Washington Streets on the Freedom Trail. The list that follows is selective.

About Boston, by David McCord. Little, Brown, 1973. $8.95.

A.I.A. Guide to Boston, by Michael and Susan Southworth (Boston Society of Architects). Globe Pequot Press, 1984. $14.95.

AMC Guide to Country Walks Near Boston, by Alan Fisher. Appalachian Mountain Club, 1986. $6.95.

AMC Guide to More Country Walks Near Boston, by William G. Scheller. Appalachian Mountain Club, 1984. $6.95.

Beacon Hill, by A. McVoy McIntyre. Little, Brown, 1975. $6.95.

Blue Guide Boston Cambridge, by John Freely. W. W. Norton, 1984. $15.95.

A Book for Boston, Llewellyn Howland, ed. Godine, 1980. $6.95. An anthology of essays, vignettes, poems, drawings, and photographs.

Boston, by Arthur S. Harris., Jr. Kodansha, 1975. $4.95.

Boston: A Topographical History, by Walter Muir Whitehill. Harvard University Press, 1968.

Boston's Freedom Trail, by Booth and Frost. Globe Pequot Press, 1981. $6.95.

Boston Globe Historic Walks in Old Boston, by John Harris. Globe Pequot Press, 1982. $9.95.

The Boston Ice Cream Lover's Guide, by Yadin Kaufman and Lori Banov Kaufman. Addison-Wesley, 1985. $5.95.

Boston in Color, by Stewart D. McBride. Hastings House, 1977. $8.95.

Boston Looks Seaward: The Story of the Port, 1630-1940. From the WPA Federal Writers' Project. Northeastern University Press, 1985. $9.95.

Boston People's Yellow Pages. 1986. $4.95. A resource guide covering many areas.

Boston Sports Trivia, by Bernard Corbett. Quinlan Press, 1985. $7.95.

Boston Then and Now, by Peter Vanderwarker. Dover. $6.95.

Boston Trivia, by Morgan White Jr. and Bernard Corbett. Addison G. Gretchell & Son, 1984. $7.95.

Built in Boston; City and Suburb, 1800–1914, by Douglass Shand Tucci. New York Graphic Society, 1978. $23.95.

The Charles, The People's River, by Max Hall. David Godine, 1986. $12.95.

The City Observed—Boston, A Guide to the Architecture of the Hub, by Donlym Lyndon. Vintage. $7.95.

Daytripping and Dining in Southern New England, by Betsy Wittlemann and Nancy Webster. Wood Pond, 1985. $7.95.

Fodor's Boston, 1986. $7.95.

Frommer's 1985–1986 Guide to Boston. $4.95.

Geographia's Quik-Finder Boston. $2.95.

Greater Boston Park and Recreation Guide, by Mark L. Primack. Globe Pequot Press, $9.95.

Guide to Jewish Boston and New England, Steven Feldman, ed. Genesis 2, 1986. $10.95.

Guide to the Recommended Country Inns of New England, by Elizabeth Squier. Globe Pequot Press, 1985. $9.95.

Houses of Boston's Back Bay, An Architectural History, 1840–1917, by Bainbridge Bunting. Harvard University Press, 1967. $12.50.

In and Out of Boston With (or Without) Children, by Bernice Chesler. Globe Pequot Press, 1982. $9.95.

The Islands of Boston Harbor, by Edward Roue Snow. Dodd, Mead, 1984. $9.95.

Klein's Rand McNally Maps of Boston and Vicinity. $1.50.

Books

Lost Boston, by Jane Holtz Kay. Houghton Mifflin, 1980. $12.95.

To Market, to Market—Six Walking Tours of the Old and the New Boston, by Corinne Madden Ross. Charles River Books, 1980. $4.50.

Old Landmarks and Historic Personages of Boston, by Samuel Adams Drake. Tuttle, 1971. $3.95.

One Boy's Boston 1887–1901, by Samuel Eliot Morison. Northeastern University Press, 1983. $10.00.

Over Boston, Aerial Photographs, by David King Gleason. Louisiana State University Press, 1986. $34.95.

Robert Nadeau's Guide to Boston Restaurants, by Mark Zanger. World Food Press, 1978. $3.95.

Short Bike Rides in Greater Boston and Central Massachusetts, by Howard Stone. Globe Pequot Press, 1986. $8.95.

Streetcar Suburbs: The Process of Growth in Boston, 1870–1900, by Sam Bass Warner, Jr. Harvard University Press, 1962. $9.95.

Underground Marketplace: A Guide to New England and the Middle Atlantic States, by Jonathan and Harriet Webster. Universe, 1981. $6.95.

Unofficial Guide to Life at Harvard, by Harvard Student Agencies, 1986. $3.95.

Victorian Boston Today. New England Chapter of the Victorian Society, 1984. $4.95.

Where to Go and What to Do When You're Single and Living In and Around Boston, by Dale Koppel. DK Enterprises, 1985. $7.95.

Bookstores

Becauses of the many colleges and universities in the area, Boston and Cambridge have one of the highest concentrations of bookstores in the United States. The list that follows is highly selective.

Architectural Book Shop 66 Hereford Street (262-2727). Affiliated with the Boston Society of Architects.

Asian Books 12 Arrow Street, Cambridge (354-0005).

Avenue Victor Hugo 339 Newbury Street (266-7746). New and used; old magazines, secondhand comics, poetry and "little" magazines.

Barnes & Nobles 603 Boylston Street (236-1308) and 395 Washington Street (426-5502).

B. Dalton Bookseller 431 Boylston Street (247-3003) and 800 Boylston Street (437-1113). New.

Book Case 42 Church Street, Cambridge (876-0832). Tons of used paperbacks, cheap as they come.

Book Exchange 85 Charles Street (523-4960). New and used.

Brattle Book Shop 9 West Street (542-0210). Over 350,000 used and rare.

Bryn Mawr Book Store 373 Huron Avenue, Cambridge (661-1770). Used and in some cases hard-to-find books.

Buddenbrooks Back Bag Booksmith 735 Boylston Street (536-4433).

Cheng & Tsui Company 25 West Street (426-6074). East Asian books.

Doubleday Faneuil Hall Market Place (439-0196).

Esplanade Paperback 103B Charles Street (523-2361). New.

Globe Corner Book Store 3 School Street (523-6658). Large selection of books on Boston and New England.

Goodspeed's Book Shop 7 Beacon Street (523-5970). Used and rare.

Groller Book Shop 6 Plympton Street, Cambridge (547-4648). Poetry; famous haunt of poets.

Harvard Book Store Café 190 Newbury Street (536-0095). Books and food; frequent readings by local writers.

Harvard Coop 1400 Massachusetts Avenue at Harvard Square, Cambridge (492-1000). New.

Kate's Mystery Bookstore 2211 Massachusetts Avenue, Cambridge (491-2660).

Lauriat's Books Inc. 30 Franklin Street (482-2850); One Washington Mall (523-4540); the Mall at Chestnut Hill, Newton (965-1481).

Mandrake 8 Story Street, Cambridge (864-3088). Art books, architecture.

Pangloss Bookshop 65 Mount Auburn Street, Cambridge (354-4003). Used and rare.

Paperback Booksmith 753 Boylston Street (536-4433); 25 Brattle Street, Cambridge (864-2321); and 11 other locations. New books at discount prices.

Penguin Bookshop 1100 Massachusetts Avenue, Cambridge (492-4144).

Reading International 47 Brattle Street, Cambridge (864-0705). Hard cover, some paperbacks, also scholarly periodicals and magazines.

Rizzoli Bookstore & Records Copley Place (437-0700).

Schoenhof's Foreign Books 76A Mount Auburn Street, Cambridge (547-8855). Foreign new.

Science Fantasy Bookstore 8 JFK Street, Cambridge (547-5917).

Shambhala Booksellers 58 JFK Street, Cambridge (547-1317). New age books and records.

Starr Book Company 186 South Street (542-2525). Used and rare books bought and sold.

Thomas More Book Store 1352 Massachusetts Avenue, Cambridge (547-8770). Religion, philosophy, theology.

Waldenbooks 3 Center Plaza, Government Center (523-3044); 383 Washington Street (426-7035); 516 Commonwealth Avenue at Kenmore Square (267-7515).

Words Worth 30 Brattle Street, Cambridge (354-5201). New books at discount prices.

BOUTIQUES

See CLOTHING; SPECIALTY SHOPS.

BUSES

See TRANSPORTATION.

CABS

See TRANSPORTATION.

CANDY

See CHOCOLATE AND CANDY.

CARS

See RENTALS.

CERAMICS, CHINA, POTTERY, AND GLASSWARE

If you can't find what you're looking for at the major department stores or at the shops listed below, try browsing through the many boutiques and specialty stores on Newbury Street, Boylston Street, or at Faneuil Hall Marketplace.

China Fair 1638 Beacon Street, Brookline (566-2220) and 2100 Massachusetts Avenue, Cambridge (864-3050). Contemporary pottery, crystal, silverware.

Cooley's Marco Polo 424 Boylston Street (536-3826). All major lines of china.

Crate and Barrel 140 Faneuil Hall Marketplace (742-6025; 1 Copley Place (536-9400); 48 Brattle Street, Cambridge (876-6300); outlet store at 171 Huron Avenue, Cambridge (547-5938). Everything for the home.

Diane at the Parker House 60 School Street (367-9030). Major lines of china, crystal, and silverware.

Pottery Cellar 1 Faneuil Hall Marketplace (742-3211). Imported handmade pottery.

Shreve, Crump and Low 330 Boylston Street (267-9100).

Simon Pearce Charles Square, Cambridge (497-7155). Hand-blown glass from Vermont, handcrafted pottery, Irish woolens.

Williams-Sonoma Copley Place (262-3080).

CHEESE SHOPS

Al Capone Cheese Co. 72 Backstone Street (227-2692). Fresh-grated parmesan, other Italian cheeses.

Cheese Importers, Ltd. 751 Boylston Street (247-0988).

Cheese 'N' Cheer 15 Huntington Avenue (262-1213).

Doe, Sullivan Company 200 Faneuil Hall Marketplace (227-9850).
Formaggio 81 Mount Auburn Street (547-4795) and 244 Huron Avenue (354-4750), both in Cambridge.

CHILDREN AND CHILDREN'S THINGS

Clothing

Calliope At Faneuil Hall Marketplace (742-1849) and 33 Brattle Street, Cambridge (547-4027).
Infants & Toddlers Inc. 1760 Massachusetts Avenue, Cambridge (576-0675). Clothes and developmental toys.
Nounours 39 Newbury Street (266-3447).
Petit Bateau Boutique 161 Newbury Street (262-5664).
Saturday's Child 2024 Massachusetts Avenue, Cambridge (661-6402).
Zabins Clothiers Inc. 206 Charles Square, Cambridge (576-2221).

Day Care

Associated Day Care Services of Metropolitan Boston 7 Marshall Street (227-4308).
Child Care Resource Center 552 Massachusetts Avenue, Cambridge (547-9861 or 547-1063).
Children's Cooperative 1151 Massachusetts Avenue, Cambridge (497-4332).
Virginia Howard Ehrlich Day Care Center At the YWCA, 140 Clarendon Street (536-7940).

Entertainment

Check the *Boston Globe*'s Thursday "Calendar" section, the *Boston Phoenix*, or the *Boston Parents Paper*, available free at libraries and other locations, for up-to-date information.

Alternative Family Cinema At Off the Wall Cinema, 15 Pearl Street, Cambridge (354-5678). Films for children are usually scheduled for weekends and holidays.

Boston By Little Feet Boston By Foot, 77 North Washington Street (367-2345). Sixty-minute walking tours geared to children's interests. For children 8–12; must be accompanied by an adult.

Boston Children's Theater 652 Hammond Road, Brookline (277-3277). Four plays a year put on by students from the Boston Children's Theater School.

Boston Public Library At Copley Square (536-5400). Film programs for children here and at certain branches.

Boston Youth Theater Cambridge (492-5176). A group of young performers who put on lively productions, usually musicals.

Cambridge Public Library 449 Broadway (498-9080). Films for children here and at certain branches.

Children's Book Shop 237 Washington Street, Brookline Village (734-7323). Sunday-afternoon children's events during the school year.

Children's Museum 300 Congress Street, Museum Wharf (426-8855). Participatory exhibits, special Friday-night performances.

Dial-A-Story (552-7148) from 6 P.M. until 8 A.M. and whenever the Newton Junior Library is closed. The library also offers a family storytelling hour about 4 times a year at the library at 126 Vernon Street, Newton.

Le Grand David Magic Show Sundays at 3 and 8 P.M. at the Cabot Street Theater, 286 Cabot Street, Beverly (927-3677). Delightful family show.

"Make Way for Ducklings" Tour Historic Neighborhood Foundation, 90 South Street (426-1898). Walking tour that traces the route of the ducks in the children's classic, *Make Way for Ducklings*, and ends with a ride on a Swan Boat in the Public Garden. Given May 1–November 30; ages 6–12.

Puppet Showplace Theater 32 Station Street, Brookline Village (731-6400). Performances feature outstanding New England puppeteers.

Youth Concerts at Symphony Hall 251 Huntington Avenue (266-1492). Boston Symphony Orchestra concerts designed for elementary and high school age children.

Playgrounds

The two major parks in downtown Boston—the Common and the Public Garden—are not really geared for children. The **Esplanade** along the Charles River, however, has playgrounds, notably the Charlesbank Playground at the northeastern end of the Esplanade (north of the Longfellow Bridge and south of Science Park). The **North End Playground**, a couple of blocks north of Old North Church and Copp's Hill Burial Ground, and the park areas around the waterfront, near the Aquarium, are popular, well-tended play areas.

See also MUSEUMS; THINGS TO DO; TOYS; ZOOS.

CHOCOLATE AND CANDY

Aux Chocolats Ltd 1221 Avenue de Lafayette (542-1151). Handmade Swiss chocolate.
Bailey's of Boston 392 Boylston Street (266-7373); 74 Franklin Street (482-7266); 26 Temple Place (426-4560); and 21 Brattle Street, Cambridge (354-2772).
Bittersweet 1364 Beacon Street, Brookline (232-5117).
Candy World 36 JFK Street, Cambridge (492-3420).
Confetti Copley Place (247-2883).
Dairy Fresh Candies 57 Salem Street (742-2639).
Dutch Cottage 96 Charles Street (227-0447).
Fanny Farmer 3 Center Plaza (723-6201); 288 Washington Street (542-7045); at Prudential Center Plaza (536-2699); 130 Tremont Street (542-8677); 1 Avenue de Lafayette (350-7194); and 184 Alewife Brook Parkway, Cambridge (661-4963).
Fruit Orchard 59 Causeway Street (742-3743).

Chocolate

Godiva Chocolatier Copley Place (437-8490).
Stowaway Sweets 154 Atlantic Avenue, Marblehead (631-0303). Where Queen Elizabeth gets her chocolate.
Sweet Stuff 353C Faneuil Hall Marketplace (227-7560) and 5 Bennett Street, Cambridge (576-6865).
Sweet Temptation 2 Copley Place (424-0605).
Thornton's English Chocolate Shop Copley Place (437-7884).

CHURCHES
See SIGHTS WORTH SEEING.

CLOTHING

Army and Navy Stores

Army Barracks 1360–62 Cambridge Street, Cambridge (491-8443). U.S. and European surplus, camping goods.
Billy Vigor's Surplus 74 Summer Street (426-6259). Genuine government surplus as well as camping and hiking gear.
Central War Surplus 433 Massachusetts Avenue, Central Square, Cambridge (876-8512).
Kenmore Army and Navy Store 508 Commonwealth Avenue, at Kenmore Square (267-2504). Jeans, fatigues, backpacks, and the like.
Mass. Army Navy Store 895 Boylston Street (267-1559). Footwear, rainwear, clothing, and camping accessories.
Snyder's Army and Navy 557 Boylston Street (536-2433). Government surplus goods, military equipment, work clothes, and camping supplies.

Men's and Women's Apparel

The Andover Shop 23 Holyoke Street, Cambridge (876-4900). Traditional men's clothing.

Ann Taylor 18 Newbury Street (262-0763); 111 Faneuil Hall Marketplace (723-7639); and 44 Brattle Street, Cambridge (864-3720). Fashions and shoes for women.

Belle France 114 Newbury Street (267-7870). Dresses for women.

Benetton Faneuil Hall Marketplace (723-7605) and 1 Avenue de Lafayette (357-5042). Italian knitwear for men and women.

Bonwit Teller 234 Berkeley Street (267-1200). Imported and American designer fashions.

Brooks Brothers 46 Newbury Street (267-2600). Men's and women's clothing.

Burberry's 2 Newbury Street (236-1000). Trenchcoats and more.

Clothwear 52 Brattle Street, Cambridge (661-6441). Fashions by local women designers.

Gazette 118 Newbury Street (267-3215). Women's fashions.

Hakikat 1248 Massachusetts Avenue, Cambridge (864-2210). Women's fashions.

Jasmine Faneuil Hall Marketplace (742-4759) and 37A Brattle Street, Cambridge (354-6043). Women's fashions.

J. August 1320 Massachusetts Avenue, Cambridge (864-6650). Men's and women's casual wear.

Joseph A. Banks Clothiers 122 Newbury Street (536-5050). Traditional clothing for men and women.

J. Press 82 Mount Auburn Street, Cambridge (547-9886). Classic Ivy League for men.

Laura Ashley 83 Newbury Street (536-0505) and Charles Square, Cambridge (497-9387). Cotton prints from London.

The Lodge 20 Brattle Street, Cambridge (547-9626). Men's and women's casual wear.

Louis 470 Boylston Street (965-6100); 130 Faneuil Hall Marketplace (742-1200); and at the Chestnut Hill Mall (965-6100). Men's fashions.

Louis for Women Faneuil Hall Marketplace (742-1200).

Martini Carl 77 Newbury Street (247-0441). European and domestic men's and women's fashions.

Neiman-Marcus At Copley Place (536-3660). Men's and women's fashions.

Roots 419 Boylston Street (247-0700). Traditional men's and women's clothing.

Saks Fifth Avenue At Prudential Center Plaza (262-8500). Men's and women's apparel.
Serenella 134 Newbury Street (262-5568). Contemporary women's clothing.
Settebello Elegantia 8 Newbury Street (262-5280). Italian imported fashions for women.
The Talbots 458 Boylston Street (262-2981) and Charles Square, Cambridge (576-2278). Classic women's clothing.

Vintage Clothing

Arsenic & Old Lace 1743 Massachusetts Avenue, Cambridge (354-7785). Basic black from the Victorian era, 1920's 1930s.
Atalanta 1700 Massachusetts Avenue, Cambridge (661-2673). Fine collection of Edwardian, Victorian, 1920s, 1930s.
C&S Talking Machine 864 Massachusetts Avenue, Cambridge (547-4424). Dresses, also jackets, tuxedo shirts for men.
Evelyn J 118 Charles Street (367-1701). Victorian skirts, blouses, tuxedo shirts, beautiful lingerie.
High Society 273 Newbury Street (266-8957). Mostly 1950s, women and men's clothing.
Keezer's Harvard Community Exchange 221 Concord Avenue, Cambridge (547-2455). The "poor man's Brooks Brothers" and a Harvard tradition since 1895.
Oona's Experienced Clothing 1210 Massachusetts Avenue, Cambridge (491-2654). 1930s, '40s, '50s dresses, shirts, and jackets for men.
Vintage, Etc. 1796 Massachusetts Avenue, Cambridge (491-1516). Hawaiian shirts, good 1950s styles.

See also BARGAINS AND DISCOUNT STORES; CHILDREN AND CHILDREN'S THINGS; DEPARTMENT STORES; SHOES.

COFFEE AND TEA

For cappuccino, espresso, and other such delights, check out the many Italian cafés on Hanover Street on Boston's North End.

Coffee

Cambridge Country Store 1795 Massachusetts Avenue, Cambridge (868-6954). More than 20 varieties of coffee beans.

Coffee Connection 36 JFK Street, Cambridge (492-4881); 2 Faneuil Hall Marketplace (227-3821); Copley Place (353-1963); and 97 Charles Street (227-3812). Buy the beans or drink the coffee here. Light meals and desserts at the Cambridge concession.

Afternoon Tea

The delightful custom of afternoon tea is still observed at several Boston hotels from 3 P.M. until 5 P.M. They include:

Copley Plaza Hotel Copley Square (267-5300).
Four Seasons Hotel 200 Boylston Street (338-4400).
Lafayette Hotel 1 Avenue de Lafayette (451-2600).
Ritz-Carlton Hotel 15 Arlington Street (536-5700).

COPY SERVICES

Charette/Stones 44 Brattle Street, Cambridge (495-0200); 45 Batterymarch Street (542-1666); and 1033 Massachusetts Avenue, Cambridge (495-0235).
Copy Cop 815 Boylston Street (267-9267); 13 Congress Street (367-2738); 85 Franklin Street (451-0233); 260 Washington Street (367-3370); and other locations. Color copying, enlargements, and copying from slides.
C. W. Beane Copy Center 315 Massachusetts Avenue (491-6898) and 1075 Massachusetts Avenue (876-0429), both in Cambridge.
Gnomon Copy 1304 Massachusetts Avenue (491-1111); 245 Massachusetts Avenue (492-2222); 99 Mount Auburn Street (492-7767); and 1206 Massachusetts Avenue (876-7767), all in Cambridge, and 627 Commonwealth Avenue (536-6666). Cheap rates; open till midnight at 1304 Massachusetts Avenue.
Sir Speedy 827 Boylston Street (267-9711); 184 High Street (451-6491); and 44 School Street (227-2237).

Top Copy 710 Commonwealth Avenue, opposite Boston University (267-8899); 327A Huntington Avenue, opposite Northeastern University (266-8113); and 11 Holyoke Street, Cambridge (497-2358).

DANCE

Boston is a considerable dance hotbed; check the *Boston Phoenix* (weekly) or the "Calendar" section in Thursday's *Boston Globe*.

Boston Ballet Company at the Wang Center, 268 Tremont Street (542-3600). Ballet offerings both modern and classical, plus *The Nutcracker* each December.

Concert Dance Company of Boston, Watertown (923-1709). Modern dance.

Copley Square Ballet 667 Boylston Street (437-9401).

Dance Umbrella 15 Sellers Street, Cambridge (492-7578). Presents visiting dance groups to Greater Boston.

Dinosaur Dance Company 10 West Street (426-2326). Unique interpretations of classical works.

Joy of Movement Center 536 Massachusetts Avenue, Cambridge (492-4680); 542 Commonwealth Avenue (266-5643); and suburban locations. Offers the "Dance Umbrella" series of modern dance, and classes in jazz, ballet, and other forms of dance.

Mandala Folk Dance 15 Sellers Street, Cambridge (868-3641).

National Center of Afro-American Artists Dance Company 122 Elm Hill Avenue, Roxbury (442-8820).

DEPARTMENT STORES

The Harvard Cooperative Society, known as "The Coop," is not just a supply store for the academic community, but a full-fledged department store that caters to the surrounding area. Visit the original store in Harvard Square in Cambridge (1400 Massachusetts Avenue; 492-1000) or the downtown Boston branch at 1 Federal Street (536-1986). Other major department stores are conveniently located at Downtown Crossing (take the "T" to Washington) or in Back Bay within walking distance of the Prudential Center (take the "T" to Copley or Prudential). A number of new stores have recently opened at Copley Place, on the south side of Copley Square; at Lafayette Place, not far from Downtown Crossing; and at Charles Square, near Harvard Square in Cambridge.

Bloomingdale's Route 9, Newton (965-1400).

Filene's 426 Washington Street (357-2978). The "Basement" is famous for extraordinary bargains. Washington MBTA station. Also suburban locations.

Jordan Marsh Company 450 Washington Street (357-3000). Near Filene's. Also suburban locations.

Lord & Taylor 760 Boylston Street, near the Prudential Center (262-6000).

Neiman-Marcus 5 Copley Place (536-3660).

Saks Fifth Avenue at the Prudential Center (262-8500).

See also BARGAINS AND DISCOUNT STORES.

DRUGSTORES

Center Plaza Pharmacy 1 Center Plaza, Government Center (227-1445).

Colonial Drug 49 Brattle Street, Cambridge (864-2222).

CVS Pharmacy 340 Washington Street (426-1970); 112 Tremont Street (426-1440); Harvard Square, Cambridge (354-4420); and other locations.

OSCO Drug 699 Mount Auburn Street, Cambridge (661-9337), and 1616 Tremont Street, Brookline (739-1030, or 739-1011, pharmacy).

Phillips Drug Store 155 Charles Street (523-1028 or 523-4372). Open 24 hours a day.

Prudential Center Pharmacy Prudential Center Plaza (267-4100). Open 7 days a week.

EMERGENCIES

For police or fire dial 911 or Operator, or the appropriate following telephone number:
Metro Police: 523-1212; Boston Police: 247-4200
Massachusetts State Police: 566-4500
Fire Department: 442-8000 or 536-1500
Ambulance: 911
Poison Control Center: 232-2120
Medox: 542-6603 (Nurses and Home Care)
Alcohol Abuse: 426-9444 or 524-7884
Drug Abuse: 536-0279
Veneral Disease: 727-2688 or 1-800-227-8922
Rape Crisis Center: 492-7273
Dental Emergency: 969-6663
Nutrition Hotline: 1-800-322-7203
Mayor's Office Night Line: 725-4000
Personal Crisis Support: 267-9150
Suicide: 247-0220
Child at Risk Hotline: 1-800-792-5200
Parents Anonymous: 1-800-882-1250
Project Place: 267-9150
Gay Hotline: 426-9371 or 1-800-221-7044
There is a **24-hour pharmacy—Phillips Drug Store**—located at 155 Charles Street, Boston; telephone 523-1028 or 523-4372. Hospitals include the following:
Beth Israel Hospital: 735-3337
Boston City Hospital: 424-5000
Brigham and Women's Hospital: 732-5636
Cambridge City Hospital: 498-1000
Children's Hospital: 735-6611
Massachusetts Eye & Ear Hospital: 523-7900
Massachusetts General Hospital: 726-2000
New England Medical Center: 956-5566
St. Elizabeth's Hospital: 789-2666

Travelers in distress can contact the Travelers Aid Society at the following locations:
Main Office, 711 Atlantic Avenue, Boston: (617) 542-7286. Open Monday through Friday, 8:45 A.M. to 4:45 P.M.

Greyhound Bus Terminal, 10 St. James Avenue (Park Square), Boston: 542-9875. Open Monday through Saturday, 11 A.M. to 7 P.M.
Logan Airport: 567-5385. Open daily, 11:30 A.M. to 7:30 P.M.
South Station: 423-7766.

The American Automobile Association (AAA) has a main information telephone number (723-9666) and an emergency road service telephone number (723-9666), both in Boston.

The *Boston Phoenix*, during the last week of every month in its "Arts" section, has a comprehensive list of aid telephone numbers and addresses covering emergencies, hotlines, alcohol and drugs, environment, gays and lesbians, health and medical assistance, legal assistance, and men's, parents', and women's needs. The White Pages of the telephone directory for Boston also has a good listing of general information and emergency telephone numbers.

See also INFORMATION.

ETHNIC NEIGHBORHOODS

The Italian neighborhood is the **North End**; if you follow the Freedom Trail it is the area between and around Paul Revere's House and Old North Church. Hanover Street is the neighborhood's main street. The streets are jammed during the summer when there are feasts held in honor of patron saints. There is good shopping here for fresh fruits and vegetables. And of course pastries! Some places to try include Caffé Paradiso (255 Hanover Street), Caffé Pompeii (280 Hanover Street), Etna's (7 Prince Street), and Prince Pastry Shop (2A Prince Street). And pizza! Regina's (11½ Thatcher Street) and Circle Pizza (361 Hanover Street) have some of the best.

Chinatown is near the downtown shopping area. Its main streets are Essex, Beach, and Kneeland streets. The Chinese New Year is celebrated every January or February (depending on the lunar calendar). You can celebrate Chinatown's savory treats at Ho Yuen Bakery (54 Beach Street), Wai Wai Ice Cream (26 Oxford Street), and Imperial Teahouse (70 Beach Street).

South Boston has been called "America's Dublin" because of the many Irish who settled there in the 19th century. In March 1776, George Washington and his army occupied the Dorchester Heights, with the result that the British were forced to evacuate Boston. A monument marks the spot. South Boston is also known for its St. Patrick's Day Parade, complete with bands, floats, and many politicians. St. Augustine's Chapel on Dorchester Street is the oldest existing Catholic church building in the state.

The **South End** is a residential neighborhood, bounded by Columbus and Harrison avenues, that was developed in the 19th century. It is noted for its brick, bow-fronted townhouses. Some of the most elegant examples are located along Rutland Square (between Columbus Avenue and Tremont Street), and Union Park (between Tremont Avenue and Shawmut Avenue), where parts of the movie *The Bostonians* were filmed. The South End today is a mixed neighborhood of blacks, Hispanics, Lebanese, and Asians. You'll find Middle Eastern groceries and restaurants along Tremont Street and elsewhere. Stop at Charlie's Sandwich Shoppe (429 Columbus Avenue) for good ribs, corn bread, and sweet potato pie.

See also RESTAURANTS; SPECIALTY SHOPS.

EXCURSIONS FROM THE CITY

The excursions listed below are all accessible by public transportation or by organized sightseeing tour. See the TOURS section for addresses and telephone numbers of the major touring companies. For some of the sights listed, such as Minute Man National Historical Park, a car is helpful in order to get a general sense of the vicinity. Hours vary according to the season. It is best to call ahead to find out days closed and evening hours.

Brookline This suburban community is located directly west of Boston. Frederick Law Olmsted National Historic Site, 99 Warren Street (566-1689), is the home of the founder of landscape architecture in America. John Fitzgerald Kennedy National Historic Site, 83 Beals Street (566-7937), is the boyhood home of the thirty-fifth president.

Cambridge The city across the Charles River from Boston, Cambridge is the home of Harvard University and Massachusetts Institute of Technology (see UNIVERSITIES AND COLLEGES). Longfellow National Historic Site, 105 Brattle Street (876-4491), is the house that poet Henry Wadsworth Longfellow lived in. Also located on Brattle Street is Tory Row, seven 18th-century mansions built by wealthy merchants. Take the Red Line to Kendall for MIT and to Harvard Square for Harvard. The best source of information about Cambridge is the Cambridge Discovery information booth located in Harvard Square near the subway entrance. Or write Cambridge Discovery, Inc., P.O. Box 1987, Cambridge, MA 02238 (617-497-1630).

Cape Ann Located along the coast to the north of Boston, Cape Ann includes the communities of Gloucester, Rockport, Essex, and Manchester. The Cape has outstanding beaches, scenic coves, and historic fishing harbors. It is a great spot for antiques hunters and artists during the entire year. In Gloucester you might enjoy visiting the Hammond Castle Museum, a recreation of a medieval castle set on a craggy ledge. The castle is at 80 Hesperus Avenue (283-7673). For information contact the Cape Ann Chamber of Commerce, 128 Main Street, Gloucester, MA 01930.

Cape Cod Across Massachusetts Bay from Boston, Cape Cod seems like a curved arm protecting metropolitan Boston from the Atlantic Ocean. Provincetown at its northern tip has a variety of attractions and can be reached from Boston by boat or airplane, directly, or by car the long way. Most of the Cape's spectacular beaches and natural areas are under the jurisdiction

PAUL REVERE HOUSE

of Cape Cod National Seashore. The superintendent's address is South Wellfleet, MA 02663; telephone, 349-3785. The southern part of the Cape is the connection for ferries to Nantucket and Martha's Vineyard.

Deerfield Located near the geographic center of Massachusetts, Deerfield is noted for its historic mile-long street with graceful trees and old houses, surrounded by fertile meadows and bordered by the meandering Deerfield River. The town also has a museum devoted to the culture of American life in the Connecticut River Valley. For more information, contact Historic Deerfield at 413-774-5581.

Jamaica Plain Actually an area of Boston, Jamaica Plain is noted for the Arnold Arboretum, part of the city's park system and funded by Harvard University. The arrangement of plants from the North Temperate climatic region was originally designed by Frederick Law Olmsted. For more information contact Arnold Arboretum, Jamaica Plain, Boston, MA 02130; 524-1717.

Lexington and Concord Minute Man National Historical Park coordinates the sites that were important in the April 1775 battles. These include Lexington Green and Concord's North Bridge. There is a Visitor Center along Battle Road about 2 miles west of Lexington. For information on the park write to the superintendent, P.O. Box 160, Concord, MA 01742, or call 369-6993 or 484-6156. Other landmarks in the vicinity include Buckman Tavern and the Museum of Our National Heritage in Lexington; Ralph Waldo Emerson's House, two houses where Nathaniel Hawthorne lived—the Wayside and the Old Manse—the Orchard House, where Louisa May Alcott lived, and Wright's Tavern in Concord; Walden Pond, where Henry David Thoreau built his cabin in the 1840s; and Great Meadows National Wildlife Reserve.

Lowell This manufacturing city northwest of Boston is also the location of an innovative park that blends the city's history with its everyday life. Lowell National Historical Park is operated by the National Park Service in cooperation with state and city agencies. Free guided tours show Lowell as a planned industrial community of the early 1800s, when the famous Lowell "mill girls" and other ethnic groups worked there and along the Merrimack River. Additional information can be obtained from the superintendent, P.O. Box 1098, Lowell, MA 01853; 459-1000.

New Bedford Located a couple of hours' drive to the southwest of Boston, New Bedford is famous for its whaling history. There is a Whaling Museum, the Whaleman's Chapel, and a restored historic district. For information on New Bedford and its vicinity, contact the Bristol County Development Council, 154 North Main Street, Fall River, MA 02722.

Plymouth Plymouth Rock, marking the Pilgrims' landing spot in 1620, is the chief attraction of this town on the coast south of Boston. There is also a replica of the *Mayflower*, an historic district, Cranberry World (a free museum devoted to cranberry art and antiques!), and Plimoth Plantation (which recreates life in early 17th-century America). Call 746-1622 for more information.

Quincy Adams National Historic Site, on Adams Street, marks the birthplaces and residences of several generations of the famous Adams family. Information can be obtained by writing to the superintendent, P.O. Box 531, Quincy, MA 02269, or by telephone, 773-1177. Quincy is located on the South Shore a few miles from downtown Boston.

Salem The town of Salem is located on the North Shore several miles from downtown Boston. Its attractions include the Salem Maritime National Historic Site (Derby Street, Salem, MA 01970; 744-4323) with the Custom House and the wharf areas; the House of the Seven Gables (54 Turner Street; 744-0991), made famous by Nathaniel Hawthorne's novel; the Peabody Museum (East India Square; 745-9500), the oldest museum in the country, featuring maritime history, ethnology, and natural history; and the Salem Witch Museum (19½ Washington Square North; 744-1692), which brings to life the terrible episode of witch trials in the town's history.

Saugus Saugus Iron Works National Historic Site, 244 Central Street, Saugus, MA 01906 (233-0050), presents life in Puritan Massachusetts in the middle of the 17th century in the context of the colony's iron-working industry. Saugus is located a few miles north of Boston.

Sturbridge Old Sturbridge Village is New England's largest outdoor living history museum showing live village and crafts in the early 1800s on 200 acres of farmland, including a working period farm. For more information telephone 347-3362. Sturbridge is located in south-central Massachusetts, easily accessible by car from the Massachusetts Turnpike.

FLOWERS

Christophers Flowers 56 Church Street, Cambridge (661-8888).
Dutch Garden 40 Brattle Street, Cambridge (491-0660). Imported bulbs, dried arrangements, and silk flowers.
Faneuil Hall Flower Market 7 North Street (742-3966). Large greenhouse market.
Greenhouse 669 Boylston Street (437-1050). Flower shop and greenhouse.
Grower's Market 889 Memorial Drive, Cambridge (661-6194). Plants and supplies.
Plantery 132 Brookline Avenue, Cambridge (236-1725). Unusual plants at low prices.
Victorian Bouquet 53 Charles Street (367-6648). Good selection of unusual buds, including many imported.

GAY SCENE

The best resources for gay men and lesbians in Boston and the surrounding area are *Gay Community News*, published weekly and considered one of the best gay newspapers in the country, and *Gayellow Pages*, Northeast edition. *Equal Times*, described as Boston's newspaper for working women, and *Focus: A Journal for Lesbians*, have interesting features pertaining to Boston's lesbians and feminists. The *Boston Phoenix* also includes up-to-date information on events of interest to Boston area gays and gay visitors. *New England Connection*, with information on bars and nightlife, is dropped off free at many of the bars listed below.

Bars and Restaurants

Boston Eagle 520 Tremont Street (542-4494). Bar for men.

Café Amalfi 8–10 Westland Avenue (536-6396). Restaurant popular with gays.

Campus 21 Brookline Avenue, Cambridge (864-0406). Video, disco; men and women.

Chaps 27 Huntington Avenue (266-7778). Men; disco.

Club Café 209 Columbus Avenue (536-0966). Restaurant popular with gays.

Greystones 8 Kingston Street (574-9429). Women's bar.

Ideal Diner 21 Huntington Avenue (247-8249). Men and women. Open late.

Jacques 79 Broadway (338-7472). Men and women; disco.

Marquee 512 Massachusetts Avenue, Central Square, Cambridge (492-9545). Bar for women; disco.

Napoleon Club 52 Piedmont Street (338-7547). Elegant bar for men. Weekend disco.

Paradise 180 Massachusetts Avenue, Cambridge (864-4130). Bar for men. Easygoing.

Playland 21 Essex Street (338-7254). Bar, mostly men. Friendly atmosphere.

Ramrod 1254 Boylston Street (266-2986). Bar for men.

Somewhere Else 295 Franklin Street (423-7730). Community bar for women.

Spit/DV8 13 Landsdowne Street (262-2424). New wave and rock and roll. Tuesday and Sunday gay nights.

Sporter's 228 Cambridge Street (742-4084). Bar for men; disco.

1270 1270 Boylston Street (261-1257). New wave and disco; men and women.

Bookstores

Esplanade Paperback 103 Charles Street (523-2361). Quality gay literature.

Glad Day Bookshop 43 Winter Street (542-0144). Good selection of gay and lesbian books and periodicals.
New Words 186 Hampshire Street, Cambridge (876-5310). Mostly feminist.
Nova Bookstore 16 LaGrange Street (542-8687).
Red Book Store 94 Green Street, Jamaica Plain (522-1464). Radical, including feminist and antiheterosexual books and periodicals.

Cinemas

Art Cinema 204 Tremont Street (482-4661).
Friends Social Club 276 Friend Street (720-4979).

Counselling and Health Care Services

Boston Gay Hotline 426-9371 (Monday–Friday 6 P.M.–midnight).
Fenway Community Health Center 16 Haviland Street (267-7573). Nonprofit health services clinic; by appointment. Near Auditorium MBTA station.
Gay and Lesbian Counseling Service 600 Washington Street (542-5188). Nonprofit psychotherapy and alcoholism counseling.

Gyms

Metropolitan Health Club 209 Columbus Avenue (536-3006).
South End Gym 1355 A Washington Street (451-3514).

Legal Assistance

Gay and Lesbian Advocates and Defenders 100 Boylston Street (426-1350). Nonprofit. Referral and counselling.

Political, Social, and Religious Organizations

Daughters of Bilitis Boston 1151 Massachusetts Avenue, Cambridge (661-3633).

Dignity At Arlington Street Church, 355 Boylston Street (536-6518).

Gay Speakers Bureau P.O. Box 2232, Boston, MA 02107 (354-0133).

Metropolitan Community Church 131 Cambridge Street (523-7664).

GLASSWARE

See CERAMICS, CHINA, POTTERY, AND GLASSWARE.

GOURMET FOODS AND MARKETS

The best single place to go for specialty foods, cheeses, coffees/teas, breads/pastries, spices/herbs, and so forth, is Faneuil Hall Marketplace, which has a score of shops catering to gourmet interests. You will also find a variety of specialty food stores at Copley Place. Other stores are:

Bella Tia 122 Salem Street (523-9064). Italian foods.

Black Forest 1759 Massachusetts Avenue, Cambridge (661-6706).

Blumsack's 285 Harvard Street, Brookline (277-6300).

Bread and Circus 392 Harvard Street, Brookline (738-8187) and 115 Prospect Street, Cambridge (492-0070). Gourmet and natural foods.

Cambridge Country Store 1759 Massachusetts Avenue, Cambridge (868-6954). Fudge to fresh orange juice.

Cardullo's Gourmet Shop 6 Brattle Street, Cambridge (491-8888) and at the Prudential Center (536-8887).

Cremaldi's 31 Putnam Street, Cambridge (354-7969). Fresh pasta, Italian foods.

De Luca's Market 11 Charles Street (523-4343) and 239 Newbury Street (262-5990).

Formaggio 81 Mount Auburn Street, in the "Garage," Cambridge (547-4795) and 244 Huron Avenue, Cambridge (354-4750).

J. Bildner & Sons 355 Commonwealth Avenue (267-1040) and 1 Devonshire Avenue (367-1350).

Kilvert & Forbes, Ltd. Faneuil Hall Marketplace (723-6050). Gourmet delights and baked goods.

Le Jardin 248 Huron Avenue, Cambridge (492-4534).

L'Espalier's Great Food Store 443-A Boylston Street (536-6543).

Malben's 384 Boylston Street (267-1646). Everything from pâté and wine to chocolates and jelly beans.

Pasta Pronto 144 Charles Street (367-5766). Fresh pasta, other ready-made Italian dishes.

Savenor's Supermarket 92 Kirkland Street, Cambridge (547-1765). The place to find exotic meats, such as bear, venison, buffalo. Where Julia Child does her shopping.

Trio's Ravioli 222 Hanover Street (742-5726). Best fresh pasta in Boston.

See also CHEESE SHOPS; COFFEE AND TEA.

GYMS, HEALTH CLUBS, AND FITNESS CENTERS

Back Bay Nautilus Fitness Center 799 Boylston Street (437-1808).

Back Bay Racquet Club 162 Columbus Avenue (262-0660).

Bodyworks Gym for Women 53 River Street, Cambridge (576-1493).

Boston Athletic Club Inc. 653 Summer Street (269-4300).

Boston Racquet Club 10 Post Office Square (482-8811).

Cambridge Racquetball 215 First Street, Cambridge (491-8989).

The Elegant Solve Spa and fitness club at the Back Bay Hilton (536-3885).

Harvard Square Athletic Club 124 Mount Auburn Street, Cambridge (492-0041).

Joy of Movement Center 542 Commonwealth Avenue (266-5646).

Le Pli Health Spa 5 Bennett Street, Cambridge (868-8087).

Nautilus 53 Inc. 53 State Street (367-1253).

Nautilus International Inc. 215 First Street, Cambridge (864-3041).

Park Plaza Health Club 64 Arlington Street (542-6861).

Sky Club 1 Devonshire Avenue (426-1212).

Tennis & Racquet Club 939 Boylston Street (536-4630).

Woman's World Health Spa 788 Boylston Street (267-4646); 64 Staniford Street (227-4500); 2000 Massachusetts Avenue, Cambridge (491-3707); and other locations.

YMCA 316 Huntington Avenue (536-7800).

YWCA 140 Clarendon Street (536-7940).

HOSPITALS

See EMERGENCIES.

HOTELS, MOTELS, BED AND BREAKFAST

Boston

Back Bay Hilton 40 Dalton Street (236-1100). Near the Prudential Center and Hynes Auditorium. Single from $115; double from $135.

Berkeley Residence Club 40 Berkeley Street (…8850). For women only. Single $23; double $28.

Boston Park Plaza Hotel 64 Arlington Street (…2000). Overlooking the Public Garden. Single f … $95; double from $110. Weekend packages.

The Bostonian At Faneuil Hall Marketplace (523-3600). Small new luxury hotel in the heart of historic Boston. Single from $150; double from $170; suites from $215. Weekend packages.

Bradford Hotel 275 Tremont Street (426-1400). Newly refurbished; in the theater district. Single from $57; double from $67 (pre-renovation).

Chandler Inn 26 Chandler Street (482-3450 or 800-842-3450). Bed and breakfast hotel. Single from $54; double from $64.

The Colonnade 120 Huntington Avenue (424-7000). European ambiance near Copley Square. Single from $110; double from $125; weekend packages, single $95, double $135.

Copley Plaza Hotel 138 St. James Avenue at Copley Square (267-5300). One of America's finest grand hotels. Single from $115; double from $135; suite from $170.

Copley Square Hotel 47 Huntington Avenue (536-9000). Friendly and informal; home of the famous Cafe Budapest. Single from $59; double from $72. Weekend specials and "economy" packages offered.

Eliot Hotel 370 Commonwealth Avenue (267-1607). In Back Bay. Single from $65; double from $75.

Embassy Suites Hotel 400 Soldiers Field Road (783-0090 or 800-EMBASSY). All-suite new hotel with river and skyline views. Suites from $110.

57 Park Plaza Hotel–Howard Johnson 200 Stuart Street (482-1800). In downtown Boston. Single from $90; double from $100.

Four Seasons Hotel 200 Boylston Street (338-4400 or 800-268-6282). New, elegant hotel opposite the Public Garden. Single from $150; double from $170. Weekend packages from $140 per night; $110 room only on weekends.

Holiday Inn–Government Center 5 Blossom Street (742-7630). Single from $89; double from $102.

Home Away 66 Mt. Vernon Street (523-1423). Short-term furnished apartments with linen, china, kitchenware in Back Bay and Beacon Hill.

Howard Johnson Motor Lodge Fenway 1271 Boylston Street (267-8300). Near the Prudential Center, Hynes Auditorium, and Fenway Park. Single from $69; double from $79.

Howard Johnson's Howard Johnson Plaza, Dorchester (288-3030). Off the Southeast Expressway and convenient to the JFK Library and the Bayside Exposition Center. Single from $60; double from $65.

Howard Johnson's Kenmore Square 575 Commonwealth Avenue (267-3100). Near Boston University and within walking distance of Hynes Auditorium and the Prudential Center. Single from $87; double from $93.

Lafayette Hotel 1 Avenue de Lafayette (451-2600). Elegant new Swiss hotel at Downtown Crossing. Single from $140; double from $160; suites from $250. Weekend packages.

Lenox Hotel 710 Boylston Street (536-5300). Near Copley Square and the Prudential Center. Single from $79; double from $94.

Marriott Hotel Long Wharf 296 State Street (227-0800). A recently built hotel on the waterfront, only minutes away from Logan Airport and Faneuil Hall Marketplace. Single from $160; double from $180. Weekend packages.

Meridien Hotel 250 Franklin Street (451-1900). Hotel with French flair in the former Federal Reserve Bank. Single from $145; double from $165; $115 weekends.

Midtown Hotel 220 Huntington Avenue (262-1000). Located across from the Prudential Center. Single from $74; double from $79.

Milner Hotel 78 Charles Street South (426-6220). A small hotel near the theater district. Single from $38.40 (w/out bath); double from $43.88.

Northeast Hall Residence 204 Bay State Road (247-8318). Near Boston University. Open June 1 to September 1. Single $12–16; double $20–25; triple $30.

Parker House 60 School Street (227-8600). Distinguished hotel on the Freedom Trail near Boston Common. Single from $69; double from $138. $94.50 weekend.

Ramada Inn 1234 Soldiers Field Road, Brighton (254-1234). Closer to Harvard Square than Boston. Single from $79; double from $89.

Ritz-Carlton Hotel 15 Arlington Street (536-5700). Elegant hotel overlooking the Public Garden. Single from $145; double from $165.

Conran's 26 Exeter Street (266-2836).
Crate and Barrel 140 Faneuil Hall Marketplace (742-6025) and 48 Brattle Street, Cambridge (876-6300).
Joy of Cooking Lafayette Place (542-8505).
The Kitchen Faneuil Hall Marketplace, North Canopy (742-3821) and 57 JFK Street in the Galleria Mall, Cambridge (492-7677).
Kitchen Arts 161 Newbury Street (266-8701).
Placewares 351 Congress Street (451-2074); 160 Newbury Street (267-5460); and 1378 Cambridge Street, Cambridge (491-8670).
Williams-Sonoma 4 Copley Place (262-3080).

ICE CREAM

Bailey's of Boston 74 Franklin Street (482-7266); Faneuil Hall Marketplace (523-5025); 21 Brattle Street, Cambridge (354-2772); and other locations.
Baskin-Robbins 1230 Massachusetts Avenue, Cambridge (547-3131) and 541 Massachusetts Avenue, Cambridge (354-9670).
Brigham's 342 Boylston Street (247-9463); 50 Congress Street (523-9372); and other locations.
Christina's Homemade Ice Cream 1255 Cambridge Street, Cambridge (492-7021).
Emack & Bollo's 290 Newbury Street (247-8772); 1310 Massachusetts Avenue, Cambridge (497-5362); 1726 Massachusetts Avenue, Cambridge (354-8573); and 7 Babcock Street, Brookline (566-8713).
Frusen Glädjé Copley Place (262-5559).
Gelateria Giuseppe 85 Mount Auburn Street, Cambridge (491-2310).
Haagen-Dazs 123–125 Mount Vernon Street (720-1360); 67 JFK Street, Cambridge (497-6552); and 520 Commonwealth Avenue (536-1661).
Herrell's 15 Dunster Street, Cambridge (497-2179) and 20 Clinton Street (367-2474).
Il Dolce Momento 30 Charles Street (720-0477).
Kelley's Homemade Ice Cream 156 Cambridge Street (523-9785).

Steve's 95 Massachusetts Avenue (262-5262); 31 Church Street, Cambridge (497-1067); and 191 Elm Street, Somerville (628-8599).
Swensen's Ice Cream Factory Quincy Market Building (723-3635).
Toscanini's Ice Cream 899 Main Street, Cambridge (491-5877).
Tuesday's 30 Station Street, Brookline Village (566-8190).

INFORMATION

The Greater Boston Convention & Visitors bureau operates a small information center, open daily from 9 A.M. until 5 P.M., at the beginning of the Freedom Trail, on the Tremont Street side of the Boston Common; the Park Street subway station has an exit (marked "Freedom Trail") near it. Another office is located at the Prudential Center. Both information centers offer many leaflets and brochures of places of interest in Boston and the vicinity. These are free. The Information Center also sells the *Official Boston Map and Freedom Trail Guide* for $1 and *The Official Guide to Boston* for $2. Be sure to ask for the free seasonal calendar of events called "Boston by Season," as well as the "Weekend Package Guide." Also available here and in hotel lobbies is the monthly magazine *Where Boston*.

The Freedom Trail itself is operated in conjunction with the National Park Service's Boston National Historical Park, an urban park which contains many diverse units not all of which are owned by the federal government. The **Visitor Information Center** for Boston National Historical Park is located on the Freedom Trail just after the Old State House and before the Faneuil Hall-Quincy Market area. It is open daily from 9 A.M. until 5 P.M. The same variety of free leaflets and brochures is also available but of greater significance is the abundance of free and better-quality official information about the Freedom Trail, historic downtown Boston, and surrounding areas. The

National Park Service brochure for Boston National Historical Park is much better—and it's free—than the one issued by the Greater Boston Convention & Visitors Bureau. It is also more complete. Ask for supplemental brochures that deal with some of the specific units of the park: Faneuil Hall, Bunker Hill, Charlestown Navy Yard, Old South Meeting House. Other National Park Service brochures are available free of charge for other parks and monuments in the Boston area: Adams National Historic Site (in Quincy), Boston African American National Historic Site (in conjunction with the Black Heritage Trail in the Beacon Hill section of Boston), Cape Cod National Seashore, Dorchester Heights National Historic Site (in South Boston), Frederick Law Olmsted National Historic Site (in Brookline), John Fitzgerald Kennedy National Historic Site (also in Brookline), Longfellow National Historic Site (in Cambridge), Lowell National Historical Park (in Lowell), Minute Man National Historical Park (in Lexington and Concord), Salem Maritime National Historic Site (in Salem), and Saugus Iron Works National Historic Site (in Saugus).

The **Visitor Center in the Prudential Center** is at the Prudential Plaza and is open daily, from 9 A.M. to 5 P.M. It is convenient to several hotels and has the same variety of maps and free brochures as are available at the Boston Common Visitor Center.

Information requested by mail can be obtained from the following: Greater Boston Convention & Visitors Bureau, Inc., Box 490, Boston, MA 02199 (617-267-6446 for recorded information), or Superintendent, Boston National Historical Park, Charlestown Navy Yard, Boston, MA 02129.

For additional information on Boston as a place to visit, work, and study, call 800-858-0200, every day from 9 A.M. to 5 P.M., or 536-4100 for specific information.

Information pertaining to the Commonwealth (State) of Massachusetts can be obtained from the **Massachusetts Tourism Office**, Department of Commerce and Development, 100 Cambridge Street, 13th Floor. Located in the Saltonstall building of the Government Center area, the office is open Monday through Friday from 9 A.M. until 5 P.M. The telephone number is 617-727-3221. Outside Massachusetts call the toll-free number, 800-727-3221.

If you plan to extend your trip to other areas of New England, the following addresses and telephone numbers might be useful:

Connecticut Tourism Division Department of Economic Development, 210 Washington Street, Hartford, CT 06106; (203) 566-3948.
Maine Publicity Bureau State House, Augusta, ME 04333; (207) 289-2423.
New Hampshire Office of Vacation Travel P.O. Box 856, Concord, NH 03301; (603) 271-2666.
Rhode Island Department of Economic Development 7 Jackson Walkway, Providence, RI 02903; (401) 277-2601.
Vermont Travel Division 61 Elm Street, Montpelier, VT 05602; (802) 828-3236.

In New York City you can get information on the 5 New England states from the **New England Vacation Center**, 630 Fifth Avenue, New York, NY 10020. The office is located in Rockefeller Center's Concourse and is open Monday through Friday from 9 A.M. until 5 P.M. The telephone number is (212) 757-4455.

A variety of useful telephone numbers for information follow:
Boston Tourist Information: 267-6446 (recorded information) or 536-4100 (visitor services)
For Individuals with Disabilities: 727-5540
Elderly Hotline: 722-4646
Center for International Visitors: 542-8995
Chamber of Commerce Info: 367-9275
National Park Service Center: 242-5642
Massachusetts Tourist Information: 727-3201
Time and Temperature: 637-1234
Weather: 936-1234
Traffic Conditions: 722-5050
Mass Transportation: 567-5400 or 722-3200
Boston Public Library: 536-5400
Parks and Recreation: 727-5250 or 725-4886 or 725-3466
Cultural Affairs Information: 725-3911
Arts Line: 437-1660
Citizens Information Service: 727-7030
Federal Information Center: 223-7121
Public Service Complaints: 725-4000
Cambridge Chamber of Commerce: 876-4100

See also EMERGENCIES.

Information

JEWELRY

Before checking the stores listed below, be sure to browse through the many shops in the Jewelers' Buildings at 333 and 387 Washington Street, Downtown Crossing.

Boston Silver & Stone Faneuil Hall Marketplace (367-1020).

Firestone & Parsons In the Ritz-Carlton Hotel, 15 Arlington Street (266-1858). Antique and contemporary.

Folklorica 1504 Faneuil Hall Marketplace (367-1201). Fron antique and traditional to Art Nouveau and modern.

Golden Temple Emporium 1440 Massachusetts Avenue, Cambridge (661-8784). American Indian, contemporary gold.

Holmberg & Douglas 30 Newbury Street (536-0350).

Jacques Sayegh 373 Washington Street, Room 305 (542-6573). Designs, repairs, and sells fine jewelry.

John Lewis 97 Newbury Street (266-6665).

Peter Wittman Handcrafted Jewelry Faneuil Hall Marketplace (523-5416).

Sherman's 11 Bromfield Street (482-9610). Also giftware, luggage, and housewares.

Shreve, Crump and Low 330 Boylston Street (267-9100). Boston's oldest—and finest—jeweler.

Tiffany Copley Place (353-0222).

LANDMARKS

See EXCURSIONS FROM THE CITY; SIGHTS WORTH SEEING; THINGS TO DO.

LEATHER GOODS AND LUGGAGE

Beacon Leather Company 106 South Street (542-7158).

Bennett and Sons 23 Church Street, Cambridge (868-7887).

Biltmore-Green Luggage 176 Boylston Street (338-8979). Factory- and custom-made.

Bon Voyage 6 Faneuil Marketplace (523-6640).

Century Leather Inc. 123 Beach Street (542-3730).

The Coach Store 75 Newbury Street (536-2777).

Gucci Copley Place (247-7000).

Helen's Leather 110 Charles Street (742-2077). Clothing.

Leather World 1372a Beacon Street, Brookline (566-5131) and 57 JFK Street, Cambridge (661-7551). Gifts and accessories.

London Harness Company 60 Franklin Street (542-9234).

Mark Cross In the Westin Hotel, 10 Huntington Avenue at Copley Place (262-2063).

Nahas Leather 65 Charles Street (723-6176). Clothing and accessories.

Santiel Designs 36 JFK Street, Cambridge (497-0715).

Walker's Riding Apparel 122 Boylston Street (423-9050).

LECTURE SERIES

Universities, libraries, museums, and many other organizations in the Boston area sponsor lectures on a wide variety of topics. Check the *Boston Globe* "Calendar" section and the *Boston Phoenix* for listings. The following are some well-established series.

Boston Literary Hour Women's City Club of Boston, 40 Beacon Street (523-6658). Talks by current authors; admission charged.

Cambridge Forum First Parish in Cambridge, 3 Church Street (876-9644). Wednesday evenings at 8. Free. Talks on a range of current topics.

Ford Hall Forum Alumni Auditorium, Northeastern University (338-5350). One of the most famous forums in the country. Free.

Humanities Series Gasson Hall, Room 100, Boston College (552-3739 or 552-8000). Long-running and popular series organized by Father Francis Sweeney. Free.

Institute of Politics Forums John F. Kennedy School of Government, Harvard University, 79 JFK Street, Cambridge (495-1380). Featuring movers and shakers in the political arena. Free.

LIBRARIES

Boston is home to both the oldest free library in the world and the oldest private library in the United States. In addition, the area's many colleges and universities have excellent library facilities.

Boston Athenaeum 10½ Beacon Street (227-0270). An impressive collection of more than 600,000 volumes available to members and accredited researchers only. Free guided tours Tuesday and Thursday by appointment.

Boston Public Library 666 Boylston Street, Copley Square (536-5400). The reference collection is housed in the original McKim, Mead, and White building. On the ground floor, you'll find government documents, microfilmed periodicals, and newspapers from all over the world; on the second floor, the main reading room; and on the third floor, special collections of rare books, prints, and books on art and music. The 1972 addition houses the circulating collection. You need a card to check out books, but even if you don't have one, the library is worth visiting because of its art work—marble lions, and murals by John Singer Sargent and others. Open Monday, 1 P.M.–9 P.M.; Tuesday–Thursday, 9 A.M.–9 P.M.; Friday and Saturday, 9 A.M.–5 P.M.; Sunday, 2 P.M.–6 P.M. (closed Sundays in summer).

Congregational Library 14 Beacon Street (523-0470). Volumes on religious history, social problems, early New England town records. Open Monday–Friday, 9 A.M.–4:30 P.M.

LUGGAGE

See LEATHER GOODS AND LUGGAGE.

MAGAZINES

See NEWSPAPERS AND MAGAZINES.

MAPS OF THE CITY

See BOOKS AND BOOKSTORES.

MOTELS

See HOTELS AND MOTELS.

MOVIE THEATERS

Boston

Allston Cinema 214 Harvard Avenue (277-2140). Boston College trolley of the Green Line.

Beacon Hill 1 Beacon Street (723-8110). Government Center.

Boston Public Library Copley Square (536-5400, ext. 46). Repertory and special-interest film series. Green Line to Copley.

Charles 1–3 185 Cambridge Street (227-1330). Green Line to Government Center or Red Line to Charles.

Cheri 50 Dalton Street, near the Prudential Center (536-2870). Green Line to Auditorium.

Cinema 57 200 Stuart Street (482-1222). Green Line to Arlington.

Coolidge Corner 290 Harvard Street, Brookline (734-2500). Repertory and old classics. Cleveland Circle trolley of the Green Line.

Copley Place Cinema Copley Place (266-1300). First-run and foreign films, plus a special tourist attraction, "Where's Boston?"

French Library 53 Marlborough Street (266-4351). French films Friday to Sunday. Green Line to Arlington.

Goethe Institute 170 Beacon Street (262-6050). Green Line to Copley.

Museum of Fine Arts 465 Huntington Avenue (267-9300). Special series. Call for information. Arborway trolley of the Green Line.

Nickelodeon Cinemas 606 Commonwealth Avenue (424-1500). Boston College branch of the Green Line; exit at Bradford Street.

Paris 841 Boylston Street (267-8181). Green Line to Copley.

Pi Alley 237 Washington Street (227-6676). Orange or Blue Line to State.

Village Cinemas 547 VFW Parkway, West Roxbury (325-0303).

Cambridge

Brattle 40 Brattle Street (876-4226). Repertory and classics. Red Line to Harvard/Brattle.

Center Screen Carpenter Center, 24 Quincy Street (494-0200). Current foreign hits and experimental films. Red Line to Harvard Square.

Janus Cinema 57 Kennedy Street (661-3737). Red Line to Harvard Square.

Harvard Epworth Church 1555 Massachusetts Avenue (354-0837). Primarily foreign films. Red Line to Harvard Square.

Harvard Film Archive Carpenter Center for the Visual Arts, 24 Quincy Street (495-4700). Foreign and experimental. Red Line to Harvard Square.

Harvard Square Theater Church Street (661-3737). Red Line to Harvard Square.

Off the Wall Cinema 15 Pearl Street (354-5678). Avant-garde and underground. Near M.I.T. Red Line to Central.

Orson Welles Cinema 1001 Massachusetts Avenue (868-3600). Avant-garde and foreign. Red Line to Central or Harvard Square.

Sack Cinema Assembly Square 35 Middlesex Avenue, Somerville (628-7000).

MUSEUMS

The Harvard University Art Museums are open 10 A.M.–5 P.M. Monday–Saturday, and 1–5 P.M. Sunday, with $3 admission for adults. The university's natural history museums are open 9 A.M.–4:15 P.M. Monday–Saturday, and 1–4:30 P.M. Sunday. Admission is free 9–11 A.M. Saturday; otherwise it is $2 for adults.

Art

Arthur M. Sackler Museum of Harvard University 485 Broadway, Cambridge (495-7768). Take the Red Line to Harvard Square. The Sackler is Harvard's newest museum, designed by noted British architect James Stirling. It houses the university's collections of Oriental, ancient, and Islamic art.

Botanical Museum of Harvard University Oxford Street, Cambridge (495-2326). Take the Red Line to Harvard Square. The Ware Collection of glass models of plants created by Leopold and Rudolf Blaschka is one of the unique museum attractions anywhere. The glass flowers look so real you might even be tempted to smell them. Admission is $2.

Busch-Reisinger Museum of Harvard University 29 Kirkland Street, Cambridge (495-2338). Take the Red Line to Harvard Square. The collection concentrates on art from central Europe, from the medieval period to the present. Admission is $3.

DeCordova and Dana Museum and Park Sandy Pond Road, Lincoln (259-8355). Take Route 2 west to Route 128 (I-95) south, to exit 47 west (Trapelo Road); take Trapelo Road to Sandy Pond Road. Turreted museum with sculpture on exhibit outdoors, changing indoor exhibits of contemporary art. Open Tuesday–Thursday, 10 A.M.–5 P.M.; Friday, 10 A.M.–9 P.M.; Saturday and Sunday, noon–5 P.M. Adults $1.50.

Fogg Art Museum of Harvard University 32 Quincy Street, Cambridge (495-2387). Take the Red Line to "Harvard." The museum has notable works of art from Italy and France, from the Middle Ages to the impressionists. Admission is $3.

Institute of Contemporary Art 955 Boylston Street (266-5151). The Green Line's "Auditorium" station is the most convenient. The exhibits encompass all genres of contemporary art: painting, sculpture, photography, crafts, graphics, video, and "performance art." The museum is open Wednesday–Sunday, 11 A.M.–5 P.M., and Friday until 8 P.M. Admission $2 for adults.

Isabella Stewart Gardner Museum 280 The Fenway (734-1359). A short walk from the Museum of Fine Arts, the Gardner Museum is compact and sublime. Originally Mrs. Gardner's residence, the museum remains, according to her will, unchanging in its collection. And the collection is astonishing: Rembrandt, Vermeer, Titian, Raphael, Matisse, Whistler, Sargent, to name just a few. The rooms are all incredible set pieces themselves. The inner courtyard, where the flowers are changed seasonally, is covered by a skylight that filters light into this breathtaking ambience. The museum is open every day except Monday from 1 P.M. until 5:30 P.M.; on Tuesday evenings it is open until 9:30 P.M. Concerts are given in one of the upper galleries Sundays at 3 P.M., Tuesdays at 6 P.M., and Thursdays at 12:15 P.M. There is no admission charge to the museum, but a contribution of $1 is suggested.

MIT Museum 265 Massachusetts Avenue, Cambridge (253-4444). Take the Red Line to Kendall Square. The museum features changing exhibits of art and photography. It is open Monday–Friday, 9 A.M.–5 P.M., and Saturday, 10 A.M.–4 P.M. Free.

Museum of Fine Arts 465 Huntington Avenue (267-9300). Museum/Ruggles MBTA stop, on the Arborway Green Line. One of America's great museums, the Museum of Fine Arts is rich in Oriental (especially Chinese and Japanese), Classical Greek and Roman, and Egyptian art. Its collection of European paintings, notably French Impressionist, is superb. The museum is also strong in 18th- and 19th-century American art. The period rooms with furniture and decorative arts from Europe and the United States are a delight to wander through. The recently completed West Wing is used to display parts of the regular collection as well as special traveling exhibits. The museum is open Tuesday–Sunday 10 A.M.–5 P.M. and Wednesday from 10 A.M.–10 P.M. The West Wing complex is also open

Thursday and Friday 5–10 P.M. Admission is $4 to the entire museum (except when the West Wing is open separately); free on Saturdays from 10 A.M.–noon.

Museum of the National Center for Afro-American Artists 300 Walnut Avenue, Roxbury/Jamaica Plain (442-8014). Take the Orange Line to Egleston station. The museum exhibits the work of black artists in all media. It is open Tuesday–Sunday, 1–5 P.M. Admission is $1.25 for adults.

Peabody Museum of Harvard University 11 Divinity Avenue, Cambridge (495-2248). Take the Red Line to Harvard Square. The focus here is ethnology, anthropology, and archeology, notably the art of pre-Columbian America. Admission fees: $2.00 adults; $1.50 senior citizens and students; $.50 children 5–15; under 5 free.

Historical and Scientific

Commonwealth Museum Massachusetts Archives, 220 Morrissey Boulevard, Dorchester (727-9268). State history museum open Monday–Friday, 9 A.M.–5 P.M. Free admission.

Computer Museum Museum Wharf, 300 Congress Street (423-6758 or 426-2800). Take the Red Line to South Station. Exhibits show the history of the computer, from the largest vacuum-tube computer ever built to today's desktop models. Personal computers provide the opportunity to experiment with computer graphics and even musical composition. The museum is open Tuesday–Sunday, 10 A.M.–6 P.M., and Thursday and Friday, 10 A.M.–9 P.M. Admission is $4 for adults.

Harvard Semitic Museum 6 Divinity Avenue, Cambridge (495-3123). Take the Red Line to Harvard Square. Exhibits feature archaeology and photography as a means of promoting the understanding of Semitic history. The museum is open Monday–Friday, 11 A.M.–5 P.M.; Sunday, 1 P.M.–5 P.M.; closed Saturday. There is usually no admission charge, although occasionally there is a charge for special exhibits.

John Fitzgerald Kennedy Library Columbia Point on Dorchester Bay (929-4523 or 929-4567). Take the Red Line (Ashmont extension) to the Columbia station and a taxi from there, or drive south on I-93 and follow the signs. The museum features films and exhibits pertaining to the life and career of President Kennedy. Admission is $2.50 for 16 and up, $1.50 for senior citizens, free under 16.

Museum of Comparative Zoology Mineralogical and Geological Museum; and Botanical Museum—all at Harvard University—24 Oxford Street, Cambridge (495-1910 or 495-2341). Take the Red Line to Harvard Square. Admission fees: $2.00 adults, $1.50 senior citizens and students, $.50 children 5–15, under 5 free.

Museum of Science Science Park (723-2500). Nearly 400 exhibits and dioramas ranging from ice crystals and fossil dinosaurs to space capsules and seeing yourself on television. There are also displays of live animals such as snakes, rats, and birds of prey. The Green Line's "Science Park" station is the closest. The museum is open daily 9 A.M.–5 P.M., and Friday until 9 P.M. Admission is $5 for adults.

Old State House—Bostonian Society 206 Washington Street (242-5655). Oldest public building in Boston, converted into a museum of the city's history. Historical talks given on the hour. Open 9:30 A.M.–5 P.M. every day. Admission is $1.25 for adults.

Other

Children's Museum Museum Wharf, 300 Congress Street (426-8855). The South Station stop on the Red Line subway is nearby. Children and adults can learn about the world around them with "hands-on" exhibits such as Giant's Desktop, City Slice, Factory, and What If You Couldn't. The museum is open Tuesday–Sunday, 10 A.M.–5 P.M., and Friday until 9 P.M. Admission is $4 for adults, $3 for children 2–15.

MUSIC

Boston is a music lover's paradise in terms of both the quality and the variety of its offerings in classical, contemporary, and experimental music. The "Arts" section of the *Boston Phoenix* and the "Calendar" sec-

BRIG BEAVER II AT BOSTON TEA PARTY MUSEUM

tion of Thursday's *Boston Globe* are the best places to check for current information.

Chamber Music

Boston Conservatory Chamber Players 8 The Fenway, Boston, MA 02215 (536-6340).

Charles River Concerts 295 Huntington Avenue, Suite 208, Boston, MA 02115 (437-0231). Series of concerts focusing on work of young and lesser-known artists.

Empire Brass Quintet 1019 Commonwealth Avenue, Boston, MA 02215 (783-8540).

Wang Celebrity Series 31 St. James Avenue, Suite 932, Boston, MA 02116 (482-2595).

Water Music Inc. 12 Arrow Street, Cambridge, MA 02138 (876-8742). Concerts aboard summer boat tours of Boston Harbor and at other locations during the rest of the year.

Choral Groups

Boston Cecilia 1773 Beacon Street, Brookline, MA 02146 (232-4540). Concerts at Jordan Hall.

Chorus Pro Musica 645 Boylston Street, Boston, MA 02116 (267-7442).

Handel and Haydn Society 158 Newbury Street, Boston, MA 02116 (266-3605). Oldest musical society in America.

Early Music

Banchetto Musicale P.O. Box 190, Cambridge, MA 02238 (491-7282). Baroque orchestra, which performs at Jordan Hall.

Boston Camerata 25 Huntington Avenue, Boston, MA 02116 (262-2092). Medieval, Renaissance, and baroque vocal and instrumental concerts.

Boston Early Music Festival 25 Huntington Avenue (262-1240). Held every other year in late spring.

Cambridge Society for Early Music P.O. Box 136, Cambridge, MA 02238 (489-3613).

ee Concerts and Organ Recitals

Berklee College of Music 1140 Boylston Street (266-1400). Student and faculty concerts weekday afternoons and evenings.

Busch-Reisinger Museum 29 Kirkland Street, Cambridge, MA 02138 (495-2338).

Cambridge Common Sundays at 2 P.M. in summer.

City Hall Plaza Boston. Noon concerts during the summer.

Emmanuel Church of Boston (Episcopal) 13 Newbury Street (536-3355). Bach cantatas every Sunday as part of service, September–May; jazz celebrations every Sunday, November–May, 7:30 P.M.

Esplanade Concerts Hatch Shell on the Charles River Embankment. Variety of summer concerts.

Isabella Stewart Gardner Museum 280 The Fenway (734-1359). Concerts in the Tapestry Room on Tuesday at 6 P.M., Thursday at 12:15 P.M., and Sunday at 3 P.M., except July and August.

See also DANCE, NIGHTLIFE; OPERA.

New Music

Boston Musica Viva 41 Bothfeld Road, Newton, MA 02159 (969-3629). Contemporary classics and new works.

Composers in Red Sneakers 33 Richdale Avenue, Cambridge, MA 02140 (661-5776). Popular group of composers who present concerts of their own works.

Dinosaur Annex Music Ensemble 25 Huntington Avenue, Boston, MA 02116 (262-0650). Works by living composers mostly.

Orchestras and Concert Halls

Berklee Performing Center 136 Massachusetts Avenue (266-7455).

Boston Chamber Music Sanders Theater, Kirkland Street, Cambridge (536-6868).

Boston Classical Orchestra 551 Tremont Street (426-2387). Performances of baroque and classical music at Faneuil Hall.

Boston Conservatory 8 The Fenway (536-6340). Frequent concerts throughout the year.

Boston Opera Company 539 Washington Street (426-4001).

Boston Philharmonic P.O. Box 354, Boston, MA 02118 (536-4001). Directed by Benjamin Zander, with performances in Jordan Hall (Boston) and Sanders Theater (Cambridge).

Boston Pops Orchestra Symphony Hall, 301 Massachusetts Avenue (266-1492). Directed by John Williams. During the summer when the regular BSO musicians go to Tanglewood in the Berkshires, the Pops musicians play at the Hatch Shell on the Charles River Esplanade.

Boston Symphony Orchestra Symphony Hall, 301 Massachusetts Avenue (266-1492). Under the baton of Seiji Ozawa. The BSO's 2,600-seat capacity hall also hosts other performance events.

Harvard-Radcliffe Orchestra Harvard University, Cambridge (459-5730).

Jordan Hall 30 Gainsborough Street (536-2412).

Longy School of Music 27 Garden Street, Cambridge (876-0956).

MIT Symphony Orchestra MIT, Cambridge (864-6900, ext. 3210).

National Center of Afro-American Artists 122 Elm Hill Avenue, Dorchester (442-8820). The Elma Lewis School performs both musical and dance works.

New England Conservatory of Music 290 Huntington Avenue (262-1120). Performances by students and faculty members. Many good, free concerts.

Pro Arte Chamber Orchestra 104 Charles Street (661-7067). Cooperative orchestra under the direction of Larry Hill.

Sanders Theater Harvard University (495-5595).

NEWSPAPERS AND MAGAZINES

Boston has 2 daily newspapers: the *Boston Globe* and the *Boston Herald-American*. Both have Sunday editions. The *Boston Phoenix*, a weekly newspaper, is an excellent resource for cultural and social events plus timely feature articles. The *Harvard Crimson* is Cambridge's only "breakfast-table daily." The *Harvard Gazette*, a weekly publication available at the Holyoke Information Center, is a good source of information about events at the university. See also the *Cambridge Chronicle* to find out what's happening on the other side of the Charles. *Gay Community News*, for Boston's gay and lesbian community, is published weekly. The *Boston Ledger*, another weekly, focuses on items of interest to the city's residents. *The Tab* is another weekly with a large circulation.

Boston magazine, a monthly publication, previews the city's cultural, social, and sports scenes. Other magazines include *Piper Street's Cultural Guide to New England* (quarterly), *New England* (monthly, a recent entry on the scene), and *Cape Cod Life* (quarterly, with information and articles about Nantucket and Martha's Vineyard as well as Cape Cod).

Nearly all newsstands in Boston and Cambridge carry *The New York Times*, other New York City newspapers, and magazines such as *Time, Newsweek,* the *New Yorker*, and so forth. The best place for domestic and foreign periodicals is the Out-of-Town Newsstand in the center of Harvard Square, in Cambridge.

NIGHTLIFE

Boston after dark. From quiet conversation and soft music to loud laughs, loud music, and energetic dancing, you will find it in the Hub. Keep in mind, however, that the subway stops running after 1 A.M. and that taxis are often difficult to locate and tend to be expensive. The list that follows includes places offering different kinds of entertainment.

Nightlife

Cafes and Coffeehouses

Algiers 40 Brattle Street, Cambridge (492-1557). Coffeehouse that offers good conversation and no music.

Blue Parrot 123 Mount Auburn Street, Cambridge (491-1551). Coffeehouse and wine bar, without music and entertainment.

Cafe Florian 85 Newbury Street (247-7603). Coffee, tea, wine, beer, and light meals; sidewalk cafe in the summer.

Cafe Paradiso 255 Hanover Street (742-1768) and 1 Eliot Place, Cambridge (868-3240). Exotic coffees; Italian ices; pastries.

Nameless Coffeehouse 3 Church Street, Cambridge (864-1630). Folk music.

Passim's 47 Palmer Street, Cambridge (492-7679). Folk music in coffeehouse setting.

Comedy Clubs

Comedy Connection 76 Warrenton Place (391-0022). Nightly entertainment by stand-up comics.

Improv Boston 212 Hampshire Street, Cambridge (576-2306). Comedy troupe doing improvised sketches, prepared pieces, songs.

Nick's Comedy Stop 100 Warrenton Street (482-0930). Professional comedians performing Wednesday –Sunday evenings.

Stitches 969 Commonwealth Avenue (254-3939). Professional comedians with some open-mike nights, Sunday–Wednesday.

Disco, Jazz, Rock

The Channel 25 Necco Street (451-1905). Popular disco with live music, guest DJs.

The Commons Copley Place (437-1234). Top 40's by DJs; very popular with singles.

The Conservatory At the Boston Marriott Hotel, Copley Place (236-5800). Two marble dance floors with music video.

Hampshire House 84 Beacon Street (227-9600). Upstairs Friday nights, recorded rock; popular with singles.

Jack's 952 Massachusetts Avenue, Cambridge (491-7800). Rock, reggae; popular with young crowd.

Jason's 131 Clarendon Street (262-9000). Another popular disco.

Jonathan Swift's Pub 30 JFK Street, Cambridge (661-9887). Live pop, jazz, blues, rock, folk.

The Jukebox 275 Tremont Street (426-1400). 1950s and 1960s rock with "period" decor; dance contests.

Metro 15 Landsdowne Street (262-2424). Live and recorded rock.

Nine Landsdowne Street 9 Landsdowne (636-0206). Warehouse disco popular with young crowd.

The Paradise 967 Commonwealth Avenue (254-2052). Live rock and new wave. Bette Midler has performed here.

The Rat 528 Commonwealth Avenue (536-2750). Punk rock popular with students.

Regattabar At the Charles Hotel, Charles Square, Cambridge (876-7777 for concert tickets). Live jazz nightly.

Ryles 212 Hampshire Street, Cambridge (876-9330). Two floors of live jazz.

Willow Jazz Club 699 Broadway, Somerville (623-9874). Jazz.

Ethnic

Averof 1924 Massachusetts Avenue, Cambridge (354-4500). Restaurant with Middle Eastern music and belly dancing.

Black Rose 160 State Street (523-8486). Pub featuring traditional Irish singers and groups.

Cantares 15 Springfield Street, Cambridge (547-6300). Latin American restaurant with live music.

Plough and Stars 912 Massachusetts Avenue, Cambridge (492-9653). Traditional Irish music.

Purple Shamrock 1 Union Street, near Quincy Market (227-2060). Irish pub with live entertainment.

Sultan's Tent 100 Warrenton Street (482-3229). Middle Eastern and Greek food and music.

Hotel and Restaurant Bars and Lounges

Back Bay Hilton 40 Dalton Street (236-1100). *Le Papillon* is a nightclub with dancing and live music.

Bay Tower Room 60 State Street (723-1666). Dance 33 floors up overlooking Boston Harbor.

Boston Park Plaza Hotel 64 Arlington Street (426-2000). *Captain's Piano Bar.*

Boston Marriott Hotel/Long Wharf 296 State Street (227-0800). Rachel's is a popular dance spot with wide-screen video. Top 40's.

Bull and Finch Pub In the Hampshire House, 84 Beacon Street (227-9605). Setting of TV series, "Cheers."

Charley's Eating and Drinking Saloon 344 Newbury Street (266-3000). Popular Back Bay hangout. Restaurant and bar.

Copley Plaza Hotel 138 St. James Avenue at Copley Square (267-5300). The *Plaza Bar* is a formal cocktail lounge with top entertainment.

Eliot Lounge Massachusetts Avenue and Commonwealth Avenue (262-8823). Bar filled with Marathon memorabilia, popular with sports fans.

Embassy Suites Hotel 400 Soldiers Field Road (338-4400). *Sculler's Lounge* features jazz.

Friday's 26 Exeter Street (266-9040). One of the most crowded and popular bars in Boston; restaurant also.

Gallaghers 55 Congress Street (523-6080). Famous piano bar at *Truffles* inside.

Howard Johnson's Motor Lodge 575 Commonwealth Avenue (267-6059). The *Starlight Roof* offers dancing and entertainment overlooking the Charles River.

Hyatt Regency Cambridge Hotel 575 Memorial Drive, Cambridge (492-1234). *Pallysadoe Lounge* has piano and vocals nightly. The *Spinnaker*, in the revolving lounge on the roof, offers great cocktails and view.

Lenox Hotel 61 Exeter Street (536-5300). *Diamond Jim's Piano Bar.*

Parker House 60 School Street (227-8600). *The Last Hurrah* and *Parker's* are 2 popular spots. The first offers a big band sound; the second, piano music.

Prudential Center On Boylston Street (536-1776). The *Hub Cap Lounge*, 52 floors up at the Top of the Hub; drinks and dinner.

Ritz-Carlton 15 Arlington Street (536-5700). The *Ritz Bar* is Boston's most sophisticated and elegant lounge.

Royal Sonesta Hotel 5 Cambridge Parkway, Cambridge (491-3600). *Charles Bar* is an intimate lounge with entertainment.

Scotch 'n Sirloin 77 North Washington Street (723-3677). Restaurant featuring music—oldies, jazz, big band—and dancing.
Sheraton-Boston Hotel 39 Dalton Street at the Prudential Center (236-2000). *Doubles Lounge* (sophisticated and contemporary), *Third Edition* (dancing—young crowd), and *Turning Point* (piano lounge overlooking hotel's busy lobby).
Westin Hotel Copley Place (262-9600). Live band. Jazz.

See also MUSIC; RESTAURANTS.

OPERA

The Opera Company of Boston, directed by Sarah Caldwell, regularly attracts national attention and invites internationally renowned singers to perform during its winter season. The Boston Concert Opera performs opera in concert form with young international and local artists. The Lyric Opera relies on local and national talent to stage performances of light operatic works.

Gilbert and Sullivan operettas are performed by Harvard and Radcliffe students at the Agassiz Theater (732-1000) and by the Boston University Savoyards (353-3341).
Boston Concert Opera Box 459, Astor Station, Boston, MA 02123 (536-1166). Performs at Jordan Hall.
Boston Lyric Opera 11 Leon Street (267-1512). Performs at the Boston Center for the Arts, corner of Tremont and Clarendon Streets.
Opera Company of Boston 539 Washington Street (426-5300). Directed by Sarah Caldwell; performs at the Opera House (formerly the Savoy), off Boston Common. Take the Green Line to Boylston or the Orange Line to Essex.

PARKS AND NATURE PRESERVES/OUTDOOR SPORTS

The parks in downtown Boston all have special characters and historic backgrounds. The Boston Common, an open expanse in front of the State House, was used during colonial days for drilling troops, grazing cows, and, occasionally, as a site for executions. Today it's a place for summer concerts, wading or skating on the Frog Pond, picnics, or just plain sitting on the grass. The Public Garden, directly to the west, is also congenial; during the summer months you can ride the famous Swan Boats in the pond and admire the beautiful flowers. Along the Charles River, on the Boston side, is the James J. Storrow Memorial Embankment, generally referred to as **The Esplanade**. Sailboats can be rented here. The view toward Beacon Hill, especially at dusk, is extraordinary when the State House's golden dome is gloriously lit by the sunlight. The Hatch Shell in the park hosts under-the-stars summer performances by the Boston Pops Orchestra. There is a matching stretch of parkland along the Charles on the Cambridge side. Both banks give you the chance to watch crew teams or rowers in individual sculls, or to see sailboats, motorboats, rowboats, and kayaks on the river. The recently redeveloped Waterfront area, directly east of Faneuil Hall Market Place, retains a parklike atmosphere because of its grassy areas and sea breezes.

The "Emerald Necklace" consists of a string of green areas running from Kenmore Square to Charlesgate, to the Back Bay Fens, to the Riverway, to the Jamaicaway, and on to the Arnold Arboretum—all designed in the 19th century by Frederick Law Olmsted. It includes the **Back Bay Fens**, Former Back Bay marshes converted into a city park with trees, grass, formal rose gardens, and some former Victory gardens that are still tended; **Olmsted Park**, along the Riverway and Jamaicaway; and **Franklin Park**, the final and largest link in the necklace, which includes a zoo and a golf course. The 265 acres of the *Arnold Arboretum* contain over 6,000 species of plants, flowers, shrubs, and trees. The arboretum is operated jointly by Harvard University and Boston's parks department. For more information telephone 524-1718.

The **Blue Hills**, to the south of Boston in Milton, are rustic enough to give you the chance to do a little mountain-climbing and hiking. There is a Trailside Museum (333-0690) with exhibits of the area's animal and plant life.

To the west of Boston is **Minute Man National Historical Park** in Lexington and Concord. Although primarily an historical park, the recreated Battle Road gives you a good sense of the countryside—except on weekends in the summer when it is very crowded. Near the park are *Walden Pond*—a state preserve that was the site of Henry David Thoreau's cabin in the 1840s, and now a lovely place to swim and hike—and *Great Meadows National Wildlife Refuge*, on the Concord River to the north of the Concord portion of Minute Man National Historical Park. Information on the park and the surrounding area can be obtained at the Visitor Center, on Battle Road about 2 miles west of Lexington, or by writing the park's superintendent (P. O. Box 160, Concord, MA 01742).

Telephone information pertaining to parks and recreation in Boston can be obtained by calling 727-5215.

Bicycling and Boating

In downtown Boston, the best bicycling area is along the Charles River on the Esplanade. Boats can be rented for use in this area at a concession located near the Hatch Shell. Community Boating, 21 Embankment Road (523-1038 or 523-9763), offers sailing instruction for adults from April to October. The Boston Sailing Center, 54 Lewis Wharf (227-4198), offers excellent week-long classes. Across the river in Cambridge the embankment area tends to be less crowded and better for bicycling. The Department of Environmental Management of Forests and Parks, 100 Cambridge Street, Boston, MA 02202 (727-3180) will send you a free pamphlet of 10 bicycle paths in the greater Boston area. The best extended path is known as the

SWAN BOAT IN PUBLIC GARDEN

Greenbelt Bikeway, a 7-mile route from the Boston Common to Franklin Park (where the zoo is). The trip takes about an hour and goes by way of the Fens and the Arnold Arboretum. There is also the Dr. Paul Dudley White Charles River Bike Path that runs along both sides of the Charles River from Watertown Square to the Museum of Science, for about 25 miles. Avoid bicycle riding on Boston's narrow, twisting, and busy streets, especially in the downtown and Beacon Hill areas. Also, the Common and the Public Garden are not very good for bicycle riding.

Camping and Hiking

Information about national, state, and local parks in the Boston vicinity can be obtained from the National Park Service Visitor Center at 15 State Street (242-5646). Two other organizations provide information about hiking and camping, as well as guided trips: the Appalachian Mountain Club, 5 Joy Street (523-0636) and the Sierra Club, 3 Joy Street (227-5339).

Running

The parklands on both sides of the Charles, in Boston and in Cambridge, are very popular with joggers from sunrise to sunset.

Skiing

In the winter there is both downhill and cross-country skiing in the nearby Blue Hills to the south of Boston in Milton. The Berkshire Mountains in western Massachusetts and the White Mountains in southern New Hampshire are close enough for a day's skiing outing; several travel companies offer 1-day, overnight, and weekend skiing packages.

Swimming

During the summer, the M.D.C. (Metropolitan District Commission) operates several outdoor swimming

Parks

pools in different locations. Call 727-5215 for information.

Both the North Shore and the South Shore are popular and crowded during the summer months. To the north, you might consider Crane's Beach at Ipswich, Plum Island in Newburyport, Manchester, Revere, Swampscott, Nahant Beach, and Marblehead; to the south, Nantasket Beach and Duxbury. These are all within easy reach of Boston. Walden Pond, near Concord, is a state preserve and offers swimming in a wooded, historical setting. Other lakes and ponds in the greater Boston area are also available for swimming. Check the YMCA and YWCA for indoor swimming.

Tennis and Racquetball

The M.D.C. (Metropolitan District Commission) operates a number of tennis courts throughout Boston. All except the Charlesbank courts are on a first-come, first-served basis. Call 523-9746 for information.

The Boston Athletic Club, 653 Summer Street (269-4300), has 7 tennis courts and 7 racquetball courts as well as complete gymnastic and health club facilities. Cambridge Racquetball, 215 First Street, Cambridge (491-8989), has 14 racquetball/hardball courts, plus sauna and steam room. Also check the YMCA and the YWCA for indoor facilities.

See also CHILDREN AND CHILDREN'S THINGS; RENTALS; SPORTS EVENTS; ZOOS.

PETS AND VETERINARY CARE

Pet Shops and Pet Supplies
Back Bay Aquarium & Pet Supplies 157 Newbury Street (262-0912).

Boston Pet Center 200 First Street, Cambridge (868-3474).

Charles Street Pet Center 250 Cambridge Street, Cambridge (523-8345).

Raining Cats & Dogs 4 Faneuil Hall Marketplace (723-2340).

Veterinary Care

Angell Memorial Animal Hospital 350 South Huntington Avenue, Jamaica Plain (522-7282).

Animal Rescue League of Boston 10 Chandler Street (426-9170).

Boston Cat Hospital 495 Park Drive (266-7877).

Brookline Animal Hospital 678 Brookline Avenue, Brookline (277-2030).

Charles Street Animal Clinic 158 Charles Street (227-0153).

Fresh Pond Animal Hospital 769 Concord Avenue, Cambridge (492-0808).

Newbury Veterinary Clinic 272 Huntington Avenue (266-9269).

PHOTOGRAPHY

See also ART GALLERIES and MUSEUMS for photography exhibits. Following is a listing of some shops with film and equipment.

Bromfield Camera & Video 10 Bromfield Street (426-5230).

Camera Center 107 State Street (227-7255). Rentals, trades, and repairs.

Claus Gelotte 284 Boylston Street (266-6366) and 185 Alewife Brook Parkway, Cambridge (868-2366).

Copley Camera Shop and HiFi Center 324 Newbury Street (266-2202)

Ferrante-Dege 1300 Massachusetts Avenue, Cambridge (547-8700).

Government Center Camera Inc. 2 Center Plaza (742-8860).

School Street Camera 280 Washington Street (423-1904).

Underground Camera 49D Prudential Center Plaza (266-5000); 638 Beacon Street (267-5336); 1 Bromfield Street (426-7811); 659 Boylston Street (266-8931); 101 First Street, Cambridge (547-4646); and 38 JFK Street, Cambridge (492-2020).

PIZZERIAS

Bel Canto 42 Charles Street on Beacon Hill (523-5575) and 928 Massachusetts Avenue, Cambridge (547-6120). Whole-wheat deep-dish crust with unusual toppings.

Bertucci's Pizza & Bocce 799 Main Street, Cambridge (661-8656); 197 Elm Street, Somerville (776-9241); and suburban locations. Pizza cooked in wood-burning brick ovens; bocce courts.

Cafe Aventura 36 JFK Street, Cambridge (491-5311).

Circle Pizza 361 Hanover Street (523-8787).

Dino's 51A Massachusetts Avenue (266-6381).

Domino's Pizza 100 Brookline Avenue, Cambridge (424-9000); 170 Tremont Street (350-0367); and suburban locations.

Pinocchio's 74 Winthrop Street, Cambridge (876-4897).

Pizzeria Uno 731 Boylston Street (267-8554) and 22 JFK Street, Cambridge (497-1530). Chicago-style thick-crust pizza.

Primo's 28 Myrtle Street (742-5458).

Regina's 11½ Thatcher Street in the North End (227-0765); Faneuil Hall Marketplace (227-8180); and 4–10 Holyoke Street, Harvard Square, Cambridge (864-9279). Best pizza at Thatcher Street location.

Ruggles 365 Washington Street (338-7981) and 1436 Massachusetts Avenue, Cambridge (497-7361).

POTTERY

See CERAMICS, CHINA, POTTERY, AND GLASSWARE.

RACETRACKS

Foxboro Raceway Also known as Bay State Raceway. About an hour southwest of Boston by car. For information call 543-5331.

Suffolk Downs Thoroughbred racing. Located about 5 miles northeast of Boston on U.S. Rte. 1. Parking is free. By subway, take the Blue Line to the Suffolk Downs station. For more information call 567-3900.

Wonderland Race Track Dog racing. Northeast of Boston, this track is accessible by the Blue Line; get out at the last stop, Wonderland. Call 284-1300 for hours and admission charges.

RADIO

See TELEVISION AND RADIO

RECORDS AND TAPES

The best place in Boston—if not in all of New England—to get records and tapes is "The Coop," that is, the Harvard Cooperative Society, 1400 Massachusetts Avenue at Harvard Square, Cambridge (492-1000). The selection is huge and the prices are good. Keep an eye out for their frequent sales. Other popular stores include the following:

Barnes & Noble 395 Washington Street (426-5502).

Boston Music Co. 116 Boylston Street (426-5100). Specializes in nostalgia records.

Briggs & Briggs 1270 Massachusetts Avenue, Cambridge (547-2007). Classical to folk and Broadway shows.

Cheapo Records 645 Massachusetts Avenue, Central Square, Cambridge (354-4455). Used and new.

Discount Records 18 JFK Street, Cambridge (492-4064).

Festoons 1154 Massachusetts Avenue, Cambridge (491-5035). Used records and tapes.

Looney Tunes 1106 Boylston Street (247-2238). Used and new.

Newbury Comics 332 Newbury Street (236-4930) and 36 JFK Street, Cambridge (491-0337). Punk, new wave, rock.

Nuggets 482 Commonwealth Avenue (536-0679) and 2201 Commonwealth Avenue (254-2202). Used jazz and rock, new releases at low prices.

Plant Records 536 Commonwealth Avenue (353-0693). New and used.

Record and Bookstore 829 Boylston Street (262-6966) and 499 Washington Street (423-7890).

Strawberries 709 Boylston Street (266-1444); 30 JFK Street, Cambridge (354-6232); and 522 Commonwealth Avenue (262-4610).

RENTALS

Bicycles

For information on routes, see PARKS AND NATURE PRESERVES.

Buck-A-Day Bicycle Leasing 20 Rawson Street (825-0741).

Community Bike Shops 490 Tremont Street (542-8623) and 175 Massachusetts Avenue, Cambridge (267-3763).

Herson Cycle Company 1250 Cambridge Street, Cambridge (876-4000).

Cars

Car rental agencies have offices at convenient locations around Boston as well as at Logan International

Airport. Some agencies have offices in the suburbs; consult the Yellow Pages for these office locations.

Ajax Rent-A-Car 161 Orleans Street, East Boston (1-800-225-AJAX).

Alamo Rent A Car 115 Bremen Street, East Boston (569-8780).

Avis Rent A Car (800-331-1212). Locations: Logan Airport (424-0800); 41 Westland Avenue, by the Prudential Center (267-5151); 61–71 High Street, in the financial district (482-6876); 3 Center Plaza (367-1190); Cambridge and suburban locations.

Brodie Auto Rentals 90 Mount Auburn Street, Cambridge (491-7600).

Budget Rent-A-Car (800-848-8005). Locations: 62 Eliot Street, at Park Square (426-2600); 1029 Commonwealth Avenue (254-0727); 350 Massachusetts Avenue, Cambridge (547-4980); and 1840 Massachusetts Avenue, Cambridge (547-0353).

Dollar Rent-A-Car (800-421-6868). Locations: Logan Airport (569-5300); 99 High Street (367-2654); Sheraton-Boston (523-5098); 1138 Massachusetts Avenue, Cambridge (354-6410).

Hertz (800-654-3131). Locations: Logan Airport (569-7272); 1 Center Plaza, near Government Center (720-0100); Motor Mart Garage, Park Square (482-9102); and 13 Holyoke Center, Cambridge (547-0336).

National Car Rental (800-328-4567). Locations: Logan Airport (569-6700); 183 Dartmouth Street (426-6830); 1663 Massachusetts Avenue, Cambridge (661-8747).

Thrifty Rent-A-Car Logan Airport (569-6500); Lewis Wharf (367-6777); Midtown Hotel, Boston (267-6633); Harvard Square, Cambridge (876-8900).

Limousines

A & A Limousine Renting 161 Broadway, Somerville (623-8700).

Beacon Hill Limousine Service Everett (387-4487). 24-hour service.

Classic Limousine Service 34 Union Park (266-3980). Restored classic sedans.

Coopers of Boston 92 State Street (482-1000). Cadillac, Rolls-Royce, Mercedes-Benz; multilingual chauffeurs.

Roller Skates

Charles River Outdoor Skate 121 Charles Street (523-9656).
Wheels 270 Newbury Street (236-1566).

See also TRANSPORTATION.

RESTAURANTS

Meals in Boston are memorable, especially if you seek out the New England specialties. Experience the hectic pace and family crowds at the famous Durgin Park. Or dine on *nouvelle cuisine* at Julien, the elegant dining room of the Hotel Meridien. The following explains our system to show approximate costs: price ranges are based on the cost of an entree only; you should assume that a 3-course dinner, with tip and tax (beverage not included) will be twice that.

$	inexpensive, under $7
$$	moderate, between $7–$12
$$$	expensive, over $12

Aegean Fare Faneuil Hall Marketplace (742-8349). Greek specialties. ($)
Another Season 97 Mount Vernon Street (367-0880). Creative Continental cuisine with changing menu. ($$)
Anthony's Pier 4 Restaurant 140 Northern Avenue (423-6363). Seafood. Good place for brunch. ($$)
Apley's In the Sheraton-Boston Hotel, 39 Dalton Street (236-2000). Split-level Continental dining. ($$$)
Ashoka Faneuil Hall Marketplace (227-6966); 39 Brattle Street, Cambridge (864-4470); and 991 Massachusetts Avenue, Cambridge (661-9001). Indian cuisine. ($$)
Aujourd'Hui In the Four Seasons Hotel, 200 Boylston Street (338-4400). French cuisine. ($$$)
Bangkok Cuisine 177a Massachusetts Avenue (262-5377). Authentic Thai cuisine. ($$–$$$)
Bay Tower Room 60 State Street (723-1666). American cuisine with seafood specialties, at 33 floors up. ($$$)

Chile's / Border Cafe

Bernardo's 24 Fleet Street (723-4554). Italian cuisine. ($$)

Bo Shek 63 Beach Street (482-4441). Chinese cuisine. ($)

Bob the Chef 604 Columbus Avenue, Roxbury (536-6204). Soul Food. ($)

Boston Park Plaza Hotel 64 Arlington Street (426-2000). Fox & Hounds Restaurant—Continental cuisine. ($$$). Café Rouge Restaurant—French bistro. ($$)

Boston Sail Loft 80 Atlantic Avenue (227-7280). American cuisine with good burgers. ($)

Buteco 130 Jersey Street, near The Fenway (247-9508). Brazilian fare. ($)

Cafe Budapest 90 Exeter Street (266-1979). Hungarian and Central European. ($$$)

Cafe Fleuri In the Hotel Meridien, 250 Franklin Street (451-1900). Continental and American cuisine in garden-court atrium.

Cafe Plaza At the Copley Plaza Hotel, 138 St. James Avenue (267-5300). French cuisine. ($$$)

Casa Romero 30 Gloucester Street (536-4341). Mexican. ($$)

China Pearl 9 Tyler Street (426-9835). Chinese cuisine. ($$)

Colonnade Hotel 120 Huntington Avenue (424-7000). Cafe Promenade—Continental cusine. ($$). Zachary's—Continental cuisine. ($$$)

Colony 384 Boylston Street (536-8500). Nouvelle American cuisine. ($$$)

Cricket's 101 Faneuil Hall Marketplace (227-3434). American cuisine. Good outdoor cafe. ($$)

Daily Catch 323 Hanover Street (523-8567). Calamari, other seafood Italian stye. ($)

Davide 326 Commercial Street (227-5745). Northern Italian. ($$)

Davio's Ristorante 269 Newbury Street (262-4810). Northern Italian cuisine. ($$)

Delmonico's In the Lenox Hotel, 710 Boylston Street (536-5300). Continental cuisine in Victorian setting. ($$$)

Dini's Sea Grill 94 Tremont Street (227-0380). Seafood. ($$)

Du Barry French Restaurant 159 Newbury Street (262-2445). French and Continental cuisines. Has good outdoor cafe. ($$)

Durgin-Park 340 Faneuil Hall Marketplace (227-2038); Copley Place (266-1964). American cuisine in an informal, famous environment. **($$)**

European Restaurant 218 Hanover Street (523-5694). Italian cuisine. **($)**

Felicia's Restaurant 145A Richmond Street (523-9885). Italian cuisine. **($$)**

57 Restaurant 200 Stuart Street (423-5700). Hearty American cuisine. **($$)**

Frogg Lane Faneuil Hall Marketplace, 2nd floor (720-0610). Mexican and American. **($)**

Front Page Eating and Drinking 29–31 Austin Street, Charlestown, at the Bunker Hill Mall (242-5010). American cuisine. **($$)**

Gallaghers 55 Congress Street (523-6080). The Dining Room—Continental and American. **($$$)**. Cafe Truffles—Lighter meals. **($$)**

Genji 327 Newbury Street (267-5656). Japanese steak house, sushi too. **($$$)**

Great Gatsby's 300 Boylston Street (536-2626). Burgers and steaks. **($)**

Hampshire House 84 Beacon Street (227-9600). Continental cuisine. **($$)**

Houlihan's Old Place 60 State Street (367-6377). International cuisine. **($$)**

Imperial Teahouse 70 Beach Street (426-8439). Chinese **($–$$)**

Jason's 131 Clarendon Street (262-9000). Continental. **($$$)**

J. C. Hillary's Ltd. 793 Boylston Street (536-6300). Steaks, burgers, and seafood. **($)**

Jimbo's Fish Shanty 245 Northern Avenue (542-5600). Regional American cuisine. **($)**

Jimmy's Harborside Restaurant 248 Northern Avenue (423-1000). Seafood. **($$)**

Joe Tecce's 53 North Washington Street (742-6210). Italian cuisine. **($$)**

Joe's American Bar/Grill 279 Dartmouth Street (536-4200). American, with huge burgers, sandwiches.

Julien In the Hotel Meridien, 1 Post Office Square (451-1900). *Nouvelle cuisine* in Frenchified former Federal Reserve Bank. **($$$)**

Kon-Tiki In the Sheraton-Boston, 39 Dalton Street (262-3063). Polynesian. **($$)**

Landmark Inn 300 Faneuil Hall Marketplace (227-9660). Bunch of Grapes—wine bar. **($)**. Flower Gar-

COPLEY SQUARE AND JOHN HANCOCK TOWERS

Cambridge

Averof Restaurant 1924 Massachusetts Avenue (354-4500). Greek and Middle Eastern cuisine. ($$)

Bartley's Burger Cottage 1246 Massachusetts Avenue (354-6559). Popular for burgers, breakfast. ($)

Bisuteki Japanese Steak House At Howard Johnson's Motor Lodge, 777 Memorial Drive (492-777). Japanese cuisine. ($$)

Brandywine Restaurant At the Sheraton Commander Hotel, 16 Garden Street (354-1234). French and Continental cuisines. ($$$)

Cajun Yankee 1193 Cambridge Street (576-7971). Trendy Cajun cuisine. ($$–$$$)

Casa Mexico 75 Winthrop Street (491-4552). Harvard Square Mexican. ($)

Casa Portugal 1200 Cambridge Street (491-8880). Pleasant Portugese, with good seafood and pork. ($)

Charles Hotel 1 Bennett Street (864-1200; 800-882-1818). The Courtyard—American cuisine in bistro setting. ($$). Rarities—seasonal Continental. ($$$)

Chez Nous 147 Huron Avenue (864-6670). French cuisine. ($$)

Ching Hua Garden 24 Holyoke Street (547-4969). Best Chinese food in Harvard Square area. ($)

East Coast Grill 1271 Cambridge Street (491-6568). American *nouvelle cuisine* in a casual setting. ($$)

Elsie's Deli 71A Mount Auburn Street (354-8362). Famous sandwiches. ($)

Harvest 44 Brattle Street (492-1115). American and Continental cuisines. ($$)

Henry IV/Ahmed's 96 Winthrop Street (876-5200). French specialties. ($$)

Hyatt Regency Cambridge Hotel 575 Memorial Drive (492-1234). Empress—Mandarin/Szechuan and Continental cuisines. ($$$). Jonah's on the Terrace—seafood. ($$). The Spinnaker—American and Continental cuisines. Good place for brunch. ($$–$$$)

Iruña 56 JFK Street (868-5633). Popular Spanish restaurant. ($$)

Joyce Chen 390 Rindge Avenue (492-7373). Chinese. ($$)

La Groceria 853 Main Street (547-9258). Italian with hot antipasto, fresh pasta. ($$)

Middle East Restaurant 4 Brookline Street (354-8238). ($$)

New Korea 1281 Cambridge Street (876-6182). Korean with specialties of barbecued beef, spicy squid. ($$)

Panache 798 Main Street (492-9500). Continental cuisine. ($$)

Peacock 5 Craigie Circle (661-4073). French provincial cuisine. ($$)

Roka 18 Eliot Street (661-0344). Japanese cuisine. ($$)

Royal Sonesta Hotel 5 Cambridge Parkway (491-3600). Toffs—seafood in Art Deco setting. ($$$). Rib Room—American and Continental cuisines. ($$$)

Tapas 2067 Massachusetts Avenue (576-2240). Continental cuisine in a 19th-century carriage building. ($$)

Upstairs at the Pudding 10 Holyoke Street (864-1933). Northern Italian prix fixe in Harvard's historic Hasty Pudding Club. ($$$)

Listing by Style

For addresses of the following restaurants, see the alphabetical listing beginning on page 80.

American Bartley's Burger Cottage, Bay Tower Room, Boston Sail Loft, Cajun Yankee, Charles Hotel—Courtyard, The Colony, Cricket's, Durgin-Park, East Coast Grill, Elsie's Deli, 57, Frogg Lane, Front Page Eating and Drinking, Gallaghers—Dining Room, Great Gatsby's, Harvest, Hyatt Regency Cambridge—Spinnaker, Landmark Inn—Wild Goose, Jimbo's Fish Shanty, Joe's American Bar/Grill, Lord Bunbury's, Newbury's Steak House, Nick's, Parker House—Parker's and The Last Hurrah, Restaurant Jasper, Royal Sonesta/Cambridge—Rib Room, Scotch 'n Sirloin, Seasons, Soupçon, Tigerlilies, Victoria Station.

Continental Another Season, Apley's, Boston Park Plaza—Fox & Hounds, Brandywine, Cafe Fleuri, Charles Hotel—Rarities, Colonnade—Cafe Promenade and Zachary's, Delmonico's, Du Barry French, Gallaghers—Dining Room, Hampshire House, Harvest, Hyatt Regency Cambridge—Empress and Spinnaker, Jason's, Landmark Inn—Wild Goose, Locke-

Ober, Medieval Manor, Panache, Parker House—Parker's, Ritz-Carlton, Royal Sonesta/Cambridge—Rib Room, St. Botolph, Tapas, Tigerlilies.

Nouvelle Cuisine (American/French) The Colony, Julien, Restaurant Jasper, Seasons.

Open-Air Crickets, Du Barry French, Maison Robert—Ben's Cafe.

Seafood Anthony's Pier 4, Bay Tower Room, Casa Portugal, Daily Catch, Dini's Sea Grill, Durgin-Park, Hyatt Regency Cambridge—Jonah's, J. C. Hillary's, Jimbo's Fish Shanty, Jimmy's Harborside, Landmark Inn—Thompson's Chowder House, The Last Hurrah, Legal Sea Foods, L'Osteria, Mass Bay, Nick's, No-Name, Royal Sonesta/Cambridge—Toff's, Salty Dog, Seaside, Top of the Hub, Union Oyster House, Winery.

Soul Food Bob the Chef.

Steak Genji, Great Gatsby's, J. C. Hillary's, Newbury's Steak House, Scotch 'n Sirloin.

View Bay Tower Room, Hyatt Regency Cambridge—Jonah's and Spinnaker, Top of the Hub.

Ethnic

Brazilian: Buteco.

Burmese: Mandalay.

Chinese: Bo Shek, China Pearl, Ching Hua Garden, Hyatt Regency Cambridge—Empress, Imperial Teahouse, Joyce Chen, Peking, Sally Ling's, Weylu's Wharf.

English: Lord Bunbury's, Medieval Manor, Olde London Pub and Grille.

French: Another Season, Aujourd'Hui, Boston Park Plaza—Café Rouge, Brandywine, Cafe Plaza, Chez Nous, Du Barry French, Henry IV/Ahmed's, Le Marquis de Lafayette, L'Espalier, Maison Robert, Peacock, Parker House—Parker's, Ritz-Carlton—Dining Room, St. Botolph, Seasons.

German: Schroeder's.

Greek: Aegean Fare, Averof.

Hungarian: Cafe Budapest.

Iberian: Casa Portugal, Iruña.

Italian: Bernardo's, Daily Catch, Davide, Davio's, European, Felicia's, Joe Tecce's, La Groceria, L'Osteria, Polcari's, Romagnoli's Table, Upstairs at the Pudding, Villa Francesca.

Indian: Ashoka.

Japanese: Bisuteki Japanese Steak House, Genji, Roka.
Korean: New Korea.
Mexican: Casa Mexico, Casa Romero, Frogg Lane, Las Brisas.
Middle Eastern: Averof, Middle East.
Polynesian: Kon-Tiki.
Thai: Bangkok Cuisine.
Vietnamese: Viet Restaurant.

SHOES

Ann Taylor 18 Newbury Street (262-1819); 111 Faneuil Hall Marketplace (723-7639); and 44 Brattle Street, Cambridge (864-3720).
Bally of Switzerland Copley Place (437-1910).
Bandolino Shoes 100 Copley Place (437-6579).
Bill Rodgers Running Center 352 Faneuil Hall Marketplace (723-5612).
Bootery of Boston 51 Temple Place (426-7699). Sizes 5–12, AAAA to EE.
Brooks Brothers 46 Newbury Street (267-2600).
Capezio Shoes Lafayette Place (357-7071).
Capezio Dance-Theater Shop 59 Temple Place (482-5825).
Cuoio 115 Newbury Street (262-0503) and Faneuil Hall Marketplace (742-4486). Italian shoes and boots.
Dance Plus 34 JFK Street, Cambridge (547-0263).
Due Mondi 272 Hanover Street (523-6097). Italian shoes and leather goods.
Edwin Case 39 Winter Street (482-5394).
Elkins Galeria of Footwear and Boutique 1218 Boylston Street, Brookline (232-2029).
Florsheim Shoes 350 Boylston Street (267-0023); 371 Washington Street (542-6639); and Avenue de Lafayette (350-6628).
George Davis Men's Shoe Company 209 Congress Street near South Station (542-2222).
J. August 1320 Massachusetts Avenue, Cambridge (864-6650). Good for running shoes and boots.

Pappagallo's 145 Newbury Street (262-3421); Copley Place (247-2532); Lafayette Place (357-7070); in the Galleria Mall at 57 JFK Street, Cambridge (876-1090); and at Faneuil Hall Marketplace (367-9026).
Tannery 400 Boylston Street (267-0899) and 11A Brattle Street, Cambridge (491-0810).
Tannery West Faneuil Hall Marketplace (723-5934) and Copley Place (424-1410).

SHOPPING MALLS

Downtown Boston has, in addition to its main commercial and shopping streets (notably Washington Street, Boylston Street, and Newbury Street—the Boston equivalent of New York's Fifth Avenue), 4 shopping centers. Much of Washington Street itself is closed to traffic, while an indoor mall has recently been opened at nearby **Lafayette Place**. Built around a courtyard, this shopping complex includes shops, restaurants, cafés, a new hotel, and a large parking garage. The **Prudential Center** is located on Boylston Street, west of Copley Square. It is dominated by the Prudential Tower and has a variety of stores ranging from a supermarket to department stores. The center is on several levels, and there is ample parking underground.

A pedestrian footbridge connects the Prudential Center to the newly opened **Copley Place**, an opulent new complex of upscale stores, hotels, and restaurants, with a 9-screen movie theater.

Faneuil Hall Marketplace, which opened a few years ago, revitalized the old Quincy Market area around Faneuil Hall. It is now Boston's most popular spot. It is located in the downtown area, adjacent to the harbor (or Waterfront, as it is more commonly called) and Government Center, directly on the Freedom Trail. There are dozens and dozens of small specialty shops that sell clothing, food, flowers, souvenirs, craft goods, antiques, books, and so forth. A large number of indoor and outdoor restaurants and cafes rang-

from informal to moderately formal are in the
ı. Parking facilities are located nearby, but during
the week parking even in garages is difficult.

See also BARGAINS AND DISCOUNT STORES; SPECIALTY
SHOPS; also individual items.

SIGHTS WORTH SEEING

Downtown Boston

Most of the historic sites in the downtown Boston area
are units of a unique urban park complex called **Boston National Historical Park**. This confederation of
historical and cultural resources is coordinated by the
National Park Service although the federal government does not actually own most of the sites. All of
the historic attractions are connected by the **Freedom
Trail**, a 3-mile-long walking tour of 16 sights and
structures in downtown Boston and across the river in
Charlestown. The landmarks include the following:

Boston Common—the oldest public park in the coun-
try.
State House—designed by Charles Bulfinch in 1795.
Park Street Church—where William Lloyd Garrison
gave his first antislavery address.
Granary Burying Ground—where John Hancock,
Sam Adams, and other patriots were buried.
King's Chapel—first Anglican church in Boston.
Benjamin Franklin Statue—site of first public school.
Old Corner Bookstore—meeting place of Longfellow,
Hawthorne, Emerson, other 19th-century literati.
South Meeting House—where the Boston Tea Party
was planned.
Old State House—seat of colonial government.
Faneuil Hall—Cradle of Liberty.
Quincy Market—built as a market for produce and
meats in the early 19th century and now restored.

Paul Revere House—oldest building in Boston.

Old North Church—where the lanterns were hung to let Paul Revere know the British were coming.

Copp's Hill Burying Ground—burial place of many early Bostonians.

Charlestown Navy Yard—home of the U.S.S. *Constitution*.

Bunker Hill Monument—site of the 1775 battle.

The National Park Service maintains a Visitor Information Center along the route between the Old State House and Faneuil Hall. A free brochure of the entire park is available as well as free brochures of some of the park's units. Some of the sites, such as Paul Revere's House, are maintained by private organizations. The Charlestown Navy Yard, where the U.S.S. *Constitution* ("Old Ironsides") is docked, and the Bunker Hill Monument are owned by the federal government. Quincy Market is a recently renovated complex of shops and restaurants that revitalizes what had been one of the busiest commercial waterfronts in the country. Faneuil Hall, often called the "Cradle of Liberty," is the building where meetings were held that initiated active protest of British colonial practices. Dorchester Heights, another unit of the park but not along the Freedom Trail, is located in South Boston; its fortification by the Americans caused the British to evacuate Boston and was the first major victory for newly appointed Commander-in-Chief George Washington. Most stops along the trail are open 10–5; in summer, some are open later.

The downtown area has other sights worth seeing in addition to those along the Freedom Trail. The **Old City Hall**—now a bank and a restaurant—located on School Street is an interesting piece of Victorian architecture. The new **City Hall**, off of Cambridge Street in Government Center, is a striking example of contemporary architecture.

The **Custom House Tower**, located on State Street, has a good view of the waterfront area from its top-floor observatory.

The Freedom Trail will take you through most of the downtown area, but you may want to wander around the waterfront itself, especially the area north of the New England Aquarium. The warehouses on Long Wharf, Commercial Wharf, and Lewis Wharf—

long abandoned—are being renovated like the nearby Quincy Market area into housing, shops, and restaurants.

Harborwalk

Boston's newest walking tour attraction, Harborwalk is a two-mile trail through the city's maritime history. A painted blue line leads from the Old State House to the Boston Tea Party Ship, passing famous sights along the way, such as the U.S. Custom House Tower, the Cunard Building, Quincy Market, Waterfront Park, Long Wharf, and the New England Aquarium. Stop by the Boston Common Information Center or the Bostix booth by Faneuil Hall for a brochure about the sites and a HarborPass, a packet of discount coupons for boat rides, museums, restaurants, and attractions along the way.

The Harbor Islands

These consist of more than 2 dozen islands, most of them included in the **Harbor Islands State Park**. Thirty-acre Georges Island has an old Civil War fort, Fort Warren, and can be reached by ferry from Long and Rowe's wharves. From there, you can take free water taxis to some of the smaller islands like Lovells, Grape, and Bumpkin, where swimming, picnicking, and hiking are allowed. For more information, write Boston Harbor Islands State Park, Building 5, Hingham, MA 02043 (749-0051).

Beacon Hill

This area of Boston with its narrow streets, brick-paved sidewalks, gas lamps, and charming old brick residences crowded next to one another is really a nationally registered historic district bounded by Beacon Street and Cambridge Street, and situated between the Charles River and Government Center. **A Black**

BOSTON WATERFRONT

OLD NORTH CHURCH

Heritage Trail connects the sites on Beacon Hill that are part of Boston African American National Historic Site. These sites include the Abiel Smith School, the first public school for black children; the Old African Meeting House, the first black Church in Boston; and the Hayden House, an important stop on the Underground Railroad. Charles Street is the main commercial street. Be sure to walk along Beacon Street with its overview of the Common. Mount Vernon Street and Pinckney Street are connected by stately Louisburg Square. The State House (open 10–4, Monday–Friday), itself at the top of the hill, was designed by Charles Bulfinch and can be toured. You might also be interested in touring one or more of these historic 19th-century houses: the Gibson House Museum, 137 Beacon Street; the Harrison Gray Otis House, 141 Cambridge Street; or the Nichols House Museum, 55 Mount Vernon Street. The streets between Charles Street and the Charles River are level ground but no less interesting than their steep neighbors. The Charles Street Meeting House is a good focal point for touring Beacon Hill.

Back Bay

Originally a marshy stretch of fens adjacent to the Charles River, Back Bay was developed in the 19th century and soon became fashionable. Commonwealth Avenue is its stately axis, but Marlborough Street is more typical of the neighborhood's quiet charm. The **Public Garden** at the eastern end is a pleasant place to dally in when the weather is nice and the flowers are in bloom. **Boylston Street**, which runs parallel to Commonwealth Avenue, is a cosmopolitan shopping area, just as busy and crowded as the Washington Street shopping area in the downtown area. **Newbury Street**, parallel to Boylston, contains many chic boutiques and art galleries. **Copley Square** is one of Boston's finest urban spaces, with a variety of architectural styles. There is Trinity Church, the Romanesque Revival masterpiece designed by Henry Hobson Richardson; the bow-fronted Copley Plaza Hotel; and the Boston Public Library, a triumph of Renaissance Revival designed by McKim, Mead, and White. These

three buildings—all built nearly a century or so ago—
are nicely complemented by the strikingly modern and
sleek John Hancock Tower (with the delightful re-
flection of Trinity Church in its steel-blue colored win-
dows) and **Copley Place** to the south. The Library's
recent addition, designed by Philip Johnson, similarly
balances the old with the new. Farther west on Boylston Street is the **Prudential Center**—another complex of office tower, hotels, stores, and the Hynes Auditorium. Another interesting and architecturally
successful group of modern structures—although just
beyond Back Bay but not quite in the developing South
End area—is the **Christian Science World Head-
quarters** along Huntington Avenue.

See also EXCURSIONS FROM THE CITY; MUSEUMS; PARKS
AND NATURE PRESERVES; THINGS TO DO.

SPECIALTY SHOPS

The list that follows is just a brief, highly selective
offering of what you can find in Boston and Cambridge. Newbury Street, Charles Street, and Faneuil
Hall Marketplace in Boston, and Harvard Square in
Cambridge are the best areas to check for unusual
items.
Alianza 140 Newbury Street (262-2385). Handcrafted
items from Latin America.
Artisans 165 Newbury Street (266-6300). Crafts from
around the world.
Audace 173 Canal Street (783-4382). Italian decorative items—marble columns, statues, terra cotta pots.
Bear Necessities 175m Faneuil Hall Marketplace
(227-2327). Bears galore.
Boston Scrimshanders 175g Faneuil Hall Marketplace
(367-1552). Scrimshaw items.
Boxes 369 Congress Street (357-8644).
Brass and Bounty 150 Faneuil Hall Marketplace (367-
1004). Brass accessories.

Brooks Gill & Co., Inc. 132 Canal Street (523-2923). Fine Oriental rugs.

Brookstone 29 School Street (742-0055); Copley Place (267-4308). Small gift items, including tools and unusual gadgets.

Celtic Weavers 175h Faneuil Hall Marketplace (720-0750). Irish handicrafts.

Copley Flair 583 Boylston Street (247-3730). Cards and small gift items.

Crabtree & Evelyn 2 Faneuil Hall Marketplace (723-7733); Copley Place (266-2778); and Charles Square, Cambridge (576-6871). Soaps, toiletries, and gourmet food items.

Decor International 171 Newbury Street (262-1529). Rugs and wall hangings from around the world.

Eiderdown Shop 229 Berkeley Street (267-6591). Quilts, down comforters, pillows, and accessories.

Eric's of Boston 38 Charles Street (227-6567). Custom framing, personalized stationery, cards, and small gift items.

Fabrications 1740 Massachusetts Avenue, Cambridge (661-6276) and 1335 Beacon Street, Brookline (731-0149). Everything for the make-it-yourselfer.

Faneuil Hall Heritage Shop 5 Faneuil Hall Marketplace (723-1776). Biggest and best selection of Boston souvenirs.

Forever Flamingo 285 Newbury Street (267-2547). Art Deco furnishings and clothing.

Gallery of Museum Shops Copley Place (267-6223). Gift items from major museums.

Goods Department Store Faneuil Hall Marketplace (367-9010) and Charles Square, Cambridge (547-2161). Trendy cards, gifts, novelties.

Have A Heart South Market of Faneuil Hall Marketplace (661-3852). Small gift items with a heart motif.

Hog Wild! 5 Faneuil Hall Marketplace (367-9520). Pigs, pigs, and more pigs.

Il Grifo 167 Newbury Street (267-9188). Unusual crafts and small gift items.

Inside Corner 99 Mount Auburn Street, Cambridge (354-7634). Stones and shells.

J. A. Parker Company 353 Faneuil Hall Marketplace (523-0128). Nautical objects and Americana.

La Ruche 174 Newbury Street (536-6366). Unusual crafts and small gift items.

Specialty Shops

Lefty Faneuil Hall Marketplace (227-7155). Everything for the left-handed person.

Little Jack Horner 169 Tremont Street (482-0219). Everything for the professional magician or practical joker.

The Melody Shop Copley Place (353-0900). Music boxes and dolls.

Peking Oriental Imports 159 Newbury Street (262-2947). Items from China.

Pierre Deux 111 Newbury Street (536-6364). Fabrics, tablecloths, shawls, dolls, and notions from Provence.

Raining Cats and Dogs Faneuil Hall Marketplace (723-2340). Gifts for dog and cat lovers.

Rayburn Musical Instrument Company 263 Huntington Avenue, next to Symphony Hall (266-4727). Boston's best.

Sharper Image Faneuil Hall Marketplace (439-0252). Robots, state-of-the-art gadgets.

Siam Malee Faneuil Hall Marketplace (227-7027). Thai silk boutique.

Silky Way 44 Kneeland Street, in Chinatown (451-5719). Oriental fashions, dishes, vases, cookware, furniture, and books.

Tissage Copley Place (267-3903). Handwoven apparel and home accessories.

Tumbleweed 99 Mount Auburn Street, in the Galeria, Cambridge (492-3279). Fabrics and craft items.

Women's Educational and Industrial Union 356 Boylston Street (536-5651). Clothing, accessories, and other handcrafted items. Great place to Christmas shop.

SPORTING GOODS

Bill Rodgers Running Center 352 Faneuil Hall Marketplace (723-5612).

Bob Smith Sporting Goods 66 Franklin Street (426-4440).

Brine's 29 Brattle Street, Cambridge (876-4218).

City Sports 168 Massachusetts Avenue (236-2222).

Eddie Bauer 510 Boylston Street (262-6700).

Fitness Shop 321 Harvard Street, Brookline (232-8659).

Herman's World of Sporting Goods 68–72 Summer Street (426-3851).

Hilton's Tent City 272 Friend Street (227-9242). Hiking, camping, skiing.

Marathon Sports 1654 Massachusetts Avenue, Cambridge (876-5816). Distance, track, and field.

Roach's Sporting Goods 1957 Massachusetts Avenue, Cambridge (876-5816). Hiking, camping, hunting, fishing.

Ski Market 860 Commonwealth Avenue (731-6100).

Tennis & Squash Shop 67A Mount Auburn Street, Cambridge (864-8800).

Walker's Riding Apparel 122 Boylston Street (423-9050).

SPORTS EVENTS

Baseball Fenway Park (267-8661) in Kenmore Square is the home of Boston's professional baseball team, the American League's **Boston Red Sox**. The season runs from early April until early October. To get to the park by subway, take the Green Line to Kenmore.

Basketball The Boston Garden (227-3200), by North Station, is where the **Celtics** play professional basketball from October to May.

Boston Marathon If you are in Boston on Patriots' Day in mid-April, you will not want to miss the annual Boston Marathon, a 26-mile running race with the finish line in front of the Hancock Tower at Copley Square. The event has attracted runners from all over the world since 1897.

Boxing and Wrestling Matches are usually held at the **Boston Garden**. For event information call 227-3200.

Football The **New England Patriots**, the Boston area's professional football team, play their home games at Sullivan Stadium in Foxboro, about 25 miles southwest of Boston. To get here, take I-93 south to Rte. 128 north; from 128 take I-95 south to Rte. 1 south. For information in Boston call 262-1776.

Head of the Charles Regatta This is another not-to-be-missed event, if you are in Boston the Sunday after Columbus Day. The regatta features 18 different events with spectators and contestants from all over the country, and from Canada as well. The race starts at the Boston University Bridge and finishes beyond Eliot Bridge.

Hockey The Boston Garden at North Station is where the **Boston Bruins** face off against visiting ice-hockey teams during the winter season. Event information at the Garden can be obtained by calling 227-3200. With all the colleges and universities in the greater Boston area there is an abundance of college sports activity. Teams from Harvard, Boston College, Boston University, Northeastern, and other local institutions engage in numerous athletic contests: hockey, basketball, soccer, baseball, rugby, track and field, to name a few. The collegiate contests that are the most popular are the fall football games, like those at Boston University's Nickerson Field, the Ivy League clashes at Harvard Stadium, and the Boston College battles with top schools from around the country. Also popular is the Boston Bean-Pot Hockey Tournament, in which Harvard, Boston College, Boston University, and Northeastern University compete. Matches are held the first and second Monday in February at the Boston Garden.

See also CHILDREN AND CHILDREN'S THINGS, GYMS AND HEALTH CLUBS, PARKS AND NATURE PRESERVES, RACETRACKS.

TEA
See COFFEE AND TEA.

TELEVISION AND RADIO

Television

In Boston the American Broadcasting Corporation (ABC) is WCVB-TV (Channel 5), the Columbia Broadcasting System (CBS) is WNEV-TV (Channel 7), the National Broadcasting Corporation (NBC) is WBZ-TV (Channel 4), and the Public Broadcasting System (PBS) is WGBH-TV (Channel 2). The daily newspapers as well as the *Boston Phoenix* list television programs.

Radio

The major AM stations:

WEEI (590)	News
WRKO (680)	Top 40
WLVG (740)	Rock, folk, disco, blues
WHDH (850)	Top 40
WBZ (1030)	Top 40; talk shows; Patriots, Celtics, and Bruins games
WILD (1090)	Soul
WEZE (1260)	Oldies
WDLW (1330)	Country
WXKS (1430)	Easy listening
WMRE (1510)	Red Sox games, talk shows, news
WUNR (1600)	Foreign languages and soul

Popular FM stations:

WMBR (88.1)	M.I.T.: multiformat, noncommercial
WERS (88.9)	Emerson College: multiformat, noncommercial
WGBH (89.7)	NPR: public, multiformat with opera, live Boston Symphony Orchestra concerts, talk shows, jazz
WBUR (90.9)	Boston University's NPR: classical, news, jazz
WBOS (92.9)	Country

WCGY (93.7)	Oldies
WZOU (94.5)	Rock, new wave
WHRB (95.3)	Harvard: commercial, nonprofit; jazz, rock, classical, news, folk, bluegrass, etc., plus extended "orgies" two times a year (for example, all of Mozart in one week)
WJIB (96.9)	Easy listening
WROR (98.5)	"Golden Great" oldies
WZLX (100.7)	Country Western
WFNX (101.7)	Rock, features by *Boston Phoenix* writers
WCRB (102.5)	Classical round-the-clock
WHTT (103.3)	Top 40
WBCN (104.1)	New wave and local bands; public service updates
WVBF (105.7)	Top 40
WMJX (106.7)	Top 40
WAAF (107.3)	Rock albums
WXKS (107.9)	"Kiss 108"—disco, adult contemporary hits

THEATERS

Boston has 5 commercial theaters that present Broadway-bound plays and musicals or road company tours of Broadway successes, or put on their own productions. These are:

Colonial Theater 106 Boylston Street (426-9366). Boylston MBTA station.

New Ehrlich Theater 551 Tremont Street (482-6316). Boylston MBTA.

Shubert Theater 265 Tremont Street (426-4520). Boylston MBTA station.

Terrace Room Boston Park Plaza Hotel, 64 Arlington Street (357-8384). Setting of the long-running Broadway musical spoof, *Forbidden Broadway*.

Wang Center for the Performing Arts 268 Tremont Street (482-9393). Home of the Boston ballet, and used for other large-scale productions in dance, opera, and drama.

Wilbur Theater 246 Tremont Street (423-4008). Boylston MBTA station.

Berklee Performance Center 136 Massachusetts Avenue (266-1400), offers, in addition to theatrical productions, contemporary arts and groups in concert.

Traditional repertory productions can be found staged at the excellent theaters in the area's colleges and universities, notably Harvard's Loeb Drama Center (in Cambridge), Tufts' Arena Theater (in Medford), Brandeis' Spingold Theater (in Waltham), the Boston University Theater, and M.I.T.'s Dramashop and Shakespeare Ensemble (in Cambridge). Of special note are the **American Repertory Theatre,** 64 Brattle Street, Cambridge (547-8300), where Robert Brustein's professional company has achieved national recognition, and the **Boston Shakespeare Company,** which offers a wide range of innovative and provocative productions. The BSC is located at 52 St. Botolph Street (267-5600). There is also the **Huntington Theater Company**, a relatively new professional repertory company under the direction of Peter Altman, which mounts productions at the Boston University Theater, 264 Huntington Avenue (266-3913). Less traditional and more unusual theaters include the following:

Alley Theater 1253 Cambridge Street, Cambridge (491-8166). New and experimental plays.

Charles Playhouse 76 Warrenton Street (426-6912). Boylston MBTA station.

Charles Playhouse Stage II 74 Warrenton Street (426-5225). Cabaret setting for Boston's longest-running comedy hit, *Shear Madness*. Boylston MBTA station.

Charlestown Working Theater 442 Bunker Hill Road, Charlestown (242-3534). Experimental.

Hasty Pudding Theater 12 Holyoke Street, Cambridge (547-3600).

Little Flags Theater 22 Sunset Street, Roxbury (232-2666). Original leftist drama.

Lyric Stage 54 Charles Street (742-8703). Charles MBTA station.

Next Move Theater 1 Boylston Street (423-5572, 423-7588). Boylston MBTA station.

Nucleo Eclettico 215 Hanover Street in the North End (367-8056).

Publick Theatre 1175 Soldiers Field Road (720-1007).

Bostix

Located at Faneuil Hall Marketplace, this centralized ticket booth and cultural information center provides tickets and information for over 100 attractions, including theater. Operated by Arts/Boston, the booth is open Tuesday–Saturday 11 A.M.–7 P.M. and Sunday noon–6 P.M. For more information, call 723-5181.

THINGS TO DO

Alexander Graham Bell Room New England Telephone Company building, first floor, 185 Franklin Street (743-9800). Bell's workshop has been reassembled to look just as it did on June 3, 1875, when he first transmitted his voice over the wires. The window of the workshop looks out over a diorama of 1875 Boston. Open Monday–Friday, 8:30 A.M.–5 P.M. Closed Saturday and Sunday. Free. Take the Red Line to South Station.

Boston Globe 135 Morrissey Boulevard, Dorchester (929-2653). Tours of a working newspaper given by appointment, Monday–Friday, 9:30 A.M., 11 A.M., 2 P.M. Children must be over 12.

Boston Tea Party Ship and Museum Congress Street Bridge on Museum Wharf (338-1773). South Station MBTA stop. The brig is a full-scale replica of one of the 3 ships that were raided in the 1773 protest. Open daily from 9 A.M. until dusk; admission is $2.25 for adults, $1.75 for children. Family and group rates available.

Bunker Hill Pavilion 55 Constitution Road (about 200 yards from the U.S.S. *Constitution*), in Charlestown Navy Yard (241-7575). Continuous showing of "Whites of Their Eyes," which recreates the 1775 battle on nearby Breed's Hill and Bunker Hill. Open daily 9:30 A.M. until 4 P.M. (6 P.M. during the summer); admission $1.50 for adults and 75¢ for children. Family, senior citizen, and group rates available.

Charles Hayden Planetarium At the Museum of Science, in Science Park (723-2500 or 742-6088). Take the Green Line subway to the Science Park station. The planetarium presents changing programs about the heavens and human exploration of them. Open daily from 9 A.M. until 4 P.M. (5 P.M. during the summer) and until 10 P.M. on Friday; admission to both Museum of Science and the Planetarium, $6.50 for adults and $4.50 for children (reduced rates on Friday evenings).

Gibson House 137 Beacon Street (267-6338). This early Back Bay residence has been preserved with all its Victorian furniture and accessories intact. Open May 1–October 31, Tuesday–Sunday, 2 P.M.–5 P.M., with tours on the hour. Take the Green Line to Arlington.

Harrison Gray Otis House 141 Cambridge Street (227-3956). The nearest subway stations are Charles Street on the Red Line and Bowdoin on the Blue Line. Designed by Charles Bulfinch (who also did the State House) in 1796, the Otis House has had a strong influence on the Federal style in New England. Open Monday through Friday by guided tours at 10, 11, 1, 2, and 3; admission is $2 for adults and $1 for children.

John Hancock Tower located at Copley Square (247-1976). The Green Line's Copley Square station is the most convenient. The Observatory on the 60th floor has, in addition to the view, a breathtaking film of the city taken from a helicopter as well as a photograph exhibit. Open daily (except Sunday) from 9 A.M. until 11 P.M.; admission is $2.75 for adults. On Sunday the Observatory opens at 10 A.M.

Mapparium In the Christian Science Publishing Society Building, at the corner of Massachusetts Avenue and Clearway Street, across from Symphony Hall (262-2300). The nearest MBTA station is Symphony on the Green Line. Walk inside a giant illuminated globe, or take a guided tour of the church, printing plant, or newsroom. Open daily (except Tuesday) 10 A.M.–5 P.M., Sunday noon–5 P.M., longer hours during the summer. Admission is free.

Nichols House 55 Mount Vernon Street (227-6993). Federal row house built when Beacon Hill was first being developed. One of the few private homes on the Hill that is open to the public, it was the lifelong home of Rose Standish Nichols, a landscape architect and world traveler. The house contains her furniture and art collection. Open Monday, Wednesday, and Saturday 1–5 P.M. Admission $1.50.

Omni Max Theater At the Museum of Science in Science Park (723-2500). Slated to open in February 1987.

Skywalk The fiftieth-floor observation deck of the Prudential Center, on Boylston Street west of Copley Square (236-3318). The Green Line stations Prudential, Copley, and Auditorium are all convenient. The Skywalk offers a 360-degree view of the city and surrounding areas. Open Monday–Thursday 9 A.M.–11 P.M., Friday and Saturday 9A.M.–midnight, Sunday 10 A.M.–11 P.M. Admission is $2 for adults, $1 for children and senior citizens; group rates available.

U.S.S. Constitution Museum At the Charlestown Navy Yard (426-1812). Although not part of the National Park Service area, the museum's exhibits are presented in conjunction with "Old Ironsides," docked a short distance away. Open daily 9 A.M.–5 P.M. during the spring and fall (until 4 P.M. during the winter, and 6 P.M. during the summer). Admission is $2 for adults and $1 for children. Group rates.

"Where's Boston?" Show and Exhibit A 50-minute multimedia introduction to the city. Open daily 10 A.M.–5 P.M. (8 P.M. during the summer); shows every hour on the hour. Admission is $3.50 for adults and $2 for children. Group rates. "Where's Boston?" is shown at the Copley Place Cinema, 100 Huntington Avenue (267-4949).

TOBACCO

David Ehrlich and Company 32 Tremont Street (227-1720) and 601 Boylston Street (266-9051).

Leavitt & Peirce, Inc. 1316 Massachusetts Avenue, Harvard Square, Cambridge (547-0576).

Lee Smoke Shop 350 Washington Street (482-2523).

L. J. Peretti Company 2½ Park Square (482-0218).

Sulgrave Ltd. The Prudential Center (267-8987); 28 State Street (523-3988); 1 Federal Street (426-4627); and other locations

TOURS

By Air
Boston Skyview, Inc. (740-4770). Helicopter flights over Boston and the North Shore coastline. $25–$75. Shuttle to the heliport from the Boston Common Information Booth.

By Boat
A. C. Cruise Line 28 Northern Avenue (426-8419). Whale watches and daily sailings to Gloucester in the summer.

Bay State Spray & Provincetown Steamship 20 Long Wharf (723-7800). Excursions to Cape Cod, around Boston Harbor, and to the Harbor Islands.

Best Tours, Inc. 11 Beacon Street (742-4265). Sightseeing cruises of Boston Harbor. Late April–early September.

Boston by Sail Lewis Wharf (742-3313). One-hour full-day cruises to the Harbor Islands.

Boston Harbor Cruises 1 Long Wharf (227-4320). Ninety-minute sightseeing tours of Boston Harbor and ferry service to George's Island. From April 1 to Columbus Day.

Massachusetts Bay Lines 398 Atlantic Avenue (542-8000). Excursions to George's Island, as well as private charters and catered clambakes.

Skyline Cruises, Inc. (523-2169). Fifty-minute trips up the Charles River from the Science Museum in summer.

Spirit of Boston 666 Summer Street (542-2974). Six-hundred-passenger cruise ship. Live entertainment.

By Bus and Trolley
Boston Doubledeckers Freedom Trail tours aboard a double-decker bus, with departures every half hour from the Boston Common Information Booth. $7 for adults, $4.50 for children under 12. Call 629-2300 for more information.

Brush Hill Transportation Company 109 Norfolk Street, Dorchester (436-4100). Historical and cultural tours of Boston and area.

Gray Line 39 Dalton Street, at the Sheraton-Boston (426-8805). Lecture tours of Boston, also of Lexington and Concord, Cape Cod, Salem, and other points in New England.

Hub Bus Lines 321 Washington Street, Somerville (776-0630). Provides sightseeing tours, chartered ski trips, and airport transfers.

Michaud Trailways 61–63 Jefferson Avenue, Salem (745-1000). America's oldest deluxe motorcoach tour carrier; from Boston to other points in New England.

Trolley Tours of Boston 329 West Second Street, South Boston (269-7010). One-hour narrated tours of the city which cover over 40 points of interest. Departures hourly 10 A.M.–6 P.M. from the harbor side of Faneuil Hall Marketplace.

Custom Tours

Boston Hosts 1313 Boylston Street (536-1800). Full range of specialized services including a multilingual guide service, harbor cruises, theme parties, and convention tours.

Boston Proper 3 Fearing Road, Hingham (749-1658). Customized tours for individuals and groups.

Exec-U-Tours of Boston 101 Blanchard Road, Cambridge (491-0118). Convention planning, historic tours, spouse programs, shuttle services, and more.

Historic Neighborhoods Foundation 90 South Street (426-1898). Guided walking tours of Beacon Hill and other neighborhoods, May through November.

New England Sights 18 Brattle Street, Cambridge (492-6689). Operates custom-designed special-interest tours throughout New England.

Travel Resources, Inc./Boston Guide Service 85 East India Wharf (367-1980). Specializes in making arrangements for groups and conventions. English and foreign language tours.

Walking Tours

Beacon Hill Garden Club Tours Walking tour of the hidden gardens of Beacon Hill, sponsored by the Beacon Hill Garden Club and held each year on a day in mid-May. Purchase tickets in advance or at different locations on Beacon Hill the day of the tour. For information, call 742-2679.

Boston By Foot 77 North Washington Street (367-2345). Walking tours of Boston, highlighting history and architecture; from April to October.

Boston Walkabouts A 64-minute cassette tape tour of the Freedom Trail, available in English, French, German, Spanish, and Japanese. Can be purchased at most Boston hotels and some giftshops and bookstores. $10.95.

Uncommon Boston Ltd. Walking tours of particular neighborhoods, plus specialized tours such as Chocolate Lovers, Halloween, etc. For information, call 266-9768.

Victorian Society in America Gibson House Museum, 137 Beacon Street (267-6338). Walking tours of different Boston neighborhoods, focusing on Victorian architecture and given on weekends in the spring and fall.

TOYS

Children's Story 434 Harvard Street, Brookline (232-6182).

Children's Workshop 1963 Massachusetts Avenue, Cambridge (354-1633).

Child World, Inc. Dedham Mall, Dedham (326-8140) and other locations. Discount.

The Dino Store 2000 Massachusetts Avenue, Cambridge (576-0702). Specializes in everything prehistoric.

F.A.O. Schwarz 40 Newbury Street (266-5101) and at the Prudential Center (266-5104).

Geppetto's Toys 5 Faneuil Hall Marketplace (367-9512).

Happiness Faneuil Hall Marketplace (742-7099). Snoopy, et al.

Henry Bear's Park 361 Huron Avenue, Cambridge (547-8424). Books, clothes, toys.

The Last Wound-Up 247 Newbury Street (424-9293).

Museum Store At the Museum of Science, Science Park (723-2500). Scientific kits and models. Also, try museum stores at the Children's Museum, 300 Congress Street, Museum Wharf (426-8855), and at the Peabody Museum of Harvard University, 11 Divinity Avenue, Cambridge (495-2248).

Name of the Game 353p Faneuil Hall Marketplace (367-1979).

Toys R Us North Shore Shopping Center, Peabody (532-9078), and other locations.

TRANSPORTATION

Subways and Trolley Buses

The Massachusetts Bay Transport Authority (MBTA) operates the subways and trolley buses. The system is the oldest in the country, dating from the 1890s; some lines still have old cars and some stations are currently under construction or renovation. The Red Line, for example, is being extended north from Harvard Square. Free MBTA maps can be obtained at the Park Street station. A more detailed map and guide to the entire system is available at the Greater Boston Convention & Visitors Bureau's Visitor Information Center on Tremont Street at the Common. Subway stations and trolley stops are marked by a large **T** inside a circle. There are 4 lines, each identified by a color. The Red Line runs north-south, from Cambridge to Mattapan or Braintree; the Blue Line runs from the northeast into the center of Boston; the Green Line has several branches running from the center of Bos-

FANEUIL HALL

ton to the west and southwest; the Orange Line is roughly a north-south line. At stations where there are 2 lines, a free transfer is possible—and the signs are quite clearly marked. The Park Street station is the main transfer point for the Red and Green lines; State Street, for the Orange and Blue lines. The fare is 60¢ by token, which may be purchased at any of the underground stations. Some lines charge an additional fare (exact change needed) for travel into areas farther from downtown Boston. The MBTA closes at 1 A.M. and has diminished service on weekends and holidays. For up-to-the-minute mass transit information call 722-3200.

Taxis

Taxis are found either cruising or at stands in Boston. Charge is on a meter basis. The current base fare upon entering a taxi is $1.10 for the first 2/7 mile, and then 20¢ for each additional 1/7 mile, and $12/hour wait time. Elderly citizens and handicapped citizens of the Boston area receive a 30% discount.

Parking

On-street parking in Boston is severely limited. There are numerous commercial zones and residents-only areas, and tickets are distributed fiercely. The rules vary around the city, and from day to day. The big parking garages under the Boston Common, in the Prudential Center, and by Quincy Market are all convenient; there are also smaller, city-owned garages in the downtown area and Back Bay, plus many privately owned establishments (whose rates are not set by the city).

Arrival in Boston

By Air

The metropolitan area is served by **Logan International Airport**, located a couple of miles to the northeast of the downtown Boston area. All flights—domestic and international—land here. Getting into Boston is easy, especially by public transportation and by the Airport Water Shuttle, which shuttles passengers from the airport to Rowes Wharf for $3. There is also a share-a-cab plan, the details of which are posted at various terminal exits.

Logan has 5 main terminals (A, B, C, D, E). The highway connecting them forms a loop, with the administration building and control tower at the far end from the airport's entrance/exit.

After claiming baggage; exit the terminal looking for signs for the free Massport Shuttle Bus. The bus connects with the subway: the Blue Line's Airport station. There are a few bus routes (not all stop at the subway station). The buses run frequently and the trip to the station takes a few minutes. The subway requires a token (60¢, purchased at the turnstile). The trip from Logan Airport to Government Center in downtown Boston takes about a half hour.

Logan Airport is the world's 10th busiest. It is located on Boston Harbor, and only rarely during the winter is it adversely affected by weather conditions. The list that follows covers most of the major airlines serving Boston; up-to-date flight information can be obtained from them.

American Airlines: 542-6700
Delta Airlines: 567-4100
Eastern Airlines: 262-3700
Midwest Express: 567-3682
New York Air: 569-8400
Northeastern: 800-327-3788
Northwest Orient: 267-4885
Pan Am: 800-223-5160
People Express: 523-0820
Piedmont: 523-1100
Republic: 482-4332
TWA: 367-2800
United: 482-7900
USAir: 482-3160

In addition, the following regional airlines provide service to vacation spots and smaller cities:
Bar Harbor Airlines (Boston to Bar Harbor): 800-732-3770

Gull Air (Hyannis to Martha's Vineyard and Nantucket): 800-222-4855

Island Air Service (Fairhaven to Cuttyhunk): 994-1231

PBA (Boston to Provincetown, Hyannis, Nantucket, Martha's Vineyard, and Burlington, VT): 567-6090

Will's Air (Boston to Hyannis and Nantucket): 800-352-7559

By Bus

There are 2 major bus terminals in Boston. Greyhound at 10 St. James Avenue, near Copley Square (423-5810), and Trailways at 55 Atlantic Avenue, near South Station (482-6620). Both terminals service state, interstate, and Canadian travel; both are near subway stations.

By Car

A good highway and street map of metropolitan Boston and the downtown area is essential to avoid getting lost, or to avoid overshooting your exit. Two interstate highways join in Boston in a general *T*-intersection. The **Massachusetts Turnpike** (I-90) runs east-west. Its eastern end is at I-93 in downtown Boston. If you are entering Boston from the west by the Mass Pike, there are 3 exits before I-90 joins with I-93. These are at the Prudential Center, Huntington Avenue, and near Tremont Street. **I-93** runs north-south through Boston. If you are coming from the south, it is called the Southeast Expressway and then the Fitzgerald Expressway; I-93 runs along the waterfront (on an elevated highway) near the Faneuil Hall-Quincy Market area. The connection with I-90 is before this area, about 1 mile south of Faneuil Hall. If you are entering Boston from the north on I-93, you cross the Charles River at Charlestown (the Charlestown Navy Yard and the U.S.S. *Constitution* will be below the bridge to the left) and, at the Fitzgerald Expressway, you pass the Faneuil Hall-Quincy Market and waterfront areas before I-93 meets with I-90. The Mass Pike (I-90) is a toll road; I-93 is not.

Once off the highway in Boston you will depend on your street map. The streets in the downtown area are narrow, curved, often one way, and occasionally blocked by construction or pedestrian zones (for example, the Freedom Trail). The same is mostly true for Beacon Hill's streets. Back Bay has a more regular geometric layout.

Access to Boston by way of **Storrow Drive** (U.S. Route 1) along the Boston side of the Charles River is clear once you are on Storrow Drive. The difficulty is getting from the Mass Pike to Storrow Drive in Allston just outside of Boston. If you come into Boston by way of Massachusetts Avenue in Cambridge, access is by the Harvard Bridge; if you stay on Main Street through downtown Cambridge, you enter Boston farther east by the Longfellow Bridge.

By Commuter Boat

Commuter boats are operated by Mass Bay Lines, 344 Atlantic Avenue (749-4500). They run between Rowe's Wharf in downtown Boston and Hewitt's Cove, off Route 3A in Hingham on the South Shore.

By Rail

Amtrak has national service from **South Station**, on Atlantic Avenue. For train arrival/departure information call the following: 482-3660 or 1-800-523-5720. The Boston and Maine Lines use **North Station**. This is primarily a commuter line that serves areas to the west and north of Boston. North Station is located at 150 Causeway Street. For information on departures and arrivals call either 227-5070 or 1-800-392-6099. Both North Station and South Station have subway stops.

UNIVERSITIES AND COLLEGES

The greater Boston area is the home of more colleges and universities than any other area in the United States. These include Tufts, Northeastern, Boston College, Boston University, Brandeis, Simmons, University of Massachusetts' Boston campus, Wellesley, Suffolk, Emerson, and Wheelock, to name a few. Two of the country's most important institutions of higher education—Harvard University and Massachusetts Institute of Technology—are located in Cambridge.

Cambridge's huge **Massachusetts Institute of Technology**, just over Harvard Bridge from Boston, has probably supplied the country with more engineers than any other institution of its kind. Many technical industries were born here. Kendall Square, north of MIT, is a beehive of high technology. Visitors to MIT are invited to wander around on their own. The Institute's Information Center, 77 Massachusetts Avenue (253-4795), issues a free brochure/map entitled "Welcome to MIT." Student-guided tours are also possible. They run just over an hour and are scheduled from 10 A.M. until 2 P.M. If you are touring on your own, don't miss Hayden Gallery in the Wiesner Building (there are usually exhibits of contemporary graphics or photography), the Hart Nautical Museum with its collection of wooden ship models, and the area around Kresge Plaza, designed by the modern architect Eero Saarinen, with Kresge Auditorium and the MIT Chapel. On the East Campus (the campus is divided into 2 parts by Massachusetts Avenue), note the high-rise Earth Science tower designed by I. M. Pei, and the huge stabile designed by Alexander Calder.

The Puritans were in the Boston area for less than 6 years when they founded Harvard College, now **Harvard University**, in Cambridge in 1636. The university has grown considerably since then from the original area to the northeast of Harvard Square. Some of the old buildings are still in use as offices and student residences. The Harvard Information Center is located at the Holyoke Center, in Harvard Square, at the corner of Massachusetts Avenue and Dunster Street (495-1573). Self-guiding material can be obtained there or guided tours can be arranged, although less easily than at MIT. North of Harvard Square are the Harvard Common and Christ Episcopal Church. Enter the campus (known as "Harvard Yard") and be sure to see Carpenter Center for the Visual Arts, the Science Center, Memorial Hall, the mammoth Widener Library, the 3 art museums—the Busch-Reisinger, the Arthur M. Sackler, and the Fogg Art Museum. In addition to the Fogg, Harvard has 4 natural history museums all located in one complex on Oxford Street. You will also want to stop by the Loeb Drama Center on Brattle Street.

Both MIT and Harvard are easily accessible from Boston by subway. Take the Red Line north to Kendall Square for MIT and Harvard Square for Harvard. If the weather is nice, you may want to walk back along the Charles River from Harvard, but keep in mind that it is a hefty hike back into downtown Boston.

WEATHER

Boston's weather is unpredictable. There tend to be long, cold, and snowy winters with fierce winds from across Massachusetts Bay. Autumn and spring are usually very pleasant but sometimes have chilly and/or rainy spells. Summers are warm, even hot. Go prepared for changing weather. The number to call for a recorded weather forecast is 936-1234.

Average Temperatures

	Day	Night
Jan.	34°F	20°F
Feb.	36°F	25°F
March	45°F	32°F
April	49°F	35°F
May	60°F	45°F
June	68°F	53°F
July	75°F	62°F
Aug.	79°F	65°F
Sept.	66°F	50°F
Oct.	60°F	48°F
Nov.	48°F	38°F
Dec.	40°F	32°F

FIRST CHURCH OF CHRIST, SCIENTIST

Suggested Clothing

Medium-weight clothing is suitable for most of the year, although light-weight garments are recommended for the summer months, and a very warm outercoat is a necessity during the winter.

WINE AND LIQUOR

Bauer Wines Co. 337 Newbury Street (262-0363).
Beacon Hill Wine & Spirits Co. Ltd. 63 Charles Street (742-8571).
Bradley Liquors 1302 Boylston Street (536-3407).
Charles Street Liquors 143 Charles Street (523-5051).
Clarendon Wine Co. 563 Boylston Street (266-6688).
Deluca's Market 11 Charles Street (523-4343) and 239 Newbury Street (262-5990).
Gloucester Wine & Spirits 299A Prudential Center Plaza (262-6571).
Harvard Provision Company 94 Mount Auburn Street, Cambridge (547-6684).
Marty's Liquors 193 Harvard Avenue, Allston (782-3250).

WOMEN'S INTERESTS

Boston and Cambridge have a large variety of organizations and events geared toward women. *Equal Times*, described as Boston's newspaper for working women, is published weekly. In the "Arts" section of the *Boston Phoenix*, also issued weekly, a lengthy column devoted to women's interests appears in the last issue of each month. Some of these events and organizations are listed below:

Aradia 520 Commonwealth Avenue (247-4861, ext. 58). Counseling center.

Boston N.O.W. (National Organization for Women) 99 Bishop Allen Drive, Cambridge (661-6015). Open house at least once a month. Consciousness raising, demonstrations.

Cambridge Women's Center 46 Pleasant Street, near Central Square, Cambridge (354-8807). Referral and resource center.

Continuum 785 Centre Street, Newton (964-3322). Private school for women who are re-entering the job market and/or changing careers. Two 22-week programs every year.

Daughters of Bilitis Boston 1151 Massachusetts Avenue, Cambridge (661-3633). Open to all women.

Glad Day Bookshop 43 Winter Street (542-0144). Boston's leading lesbian and gay bookstore.

Massachusetts Women's Political Caucus 354 Congress Street (451-9294).

New Words 186 Hampshire Street, Cambridge (876-5310). Feminist bookstore.

9 to 5 37 Temple Place (348-2970). Lobbies for better pay and better working conditions for women.

Rape Crisis Center/Hotline 492-RAPE.

Red Book Store 94 Green Street, Jamaica Plains (522-1464). Bookstore with an emphasis on feminist, Marxist, and anti-heterosexist literature.

Women's Counseling and Resource Center 1555 Massachusetts Avenue, Cambridge (492-8568).

Women's Educational and Industrial Union 356 Boylston Street (536-5651). Shop that sells clothing and handcrafted items made by women. Also, the union holds seminars for job searches, field changes, and management training.

Women's School 46 Pleasant Street, Cambridge (354-8807). Courses taught by women for women.

Women's Technical Institute 1255 Boylston Street (266-2243). Occupational technical training in electronics and drafting, as well as short course about technical careers.

YWCA 140 Clarendon Street (536-7940). The Y's Displaced Homemaker's Project is a program for women over 35 who have never worked outside the home; for information ask for extension 135. For news about other short-term workshops, classes, and special programs, ask for extension 132.

ZOOS

Franklin Park Zoo Franklin Park, on Blue Hill Avenue, Dorchester (442-0991). Just a few miles southwest of downtown Boston. Open every day from 9 A.M.– 4 P.M. (November through February), until 5 P.M. (March through October). Spread over 70 acres, the zoo contains A Bird's World, an outdoor flight cage, a waterfowl pond, and a range with exotic hooved and horned animals. There is also a tropical forest pavillion, as well as a children's zoo. Admission $1.

Walter D. Stone Memorial Zoo 149 Pond Street, Stoneham (438-3662). 7 miles north of Boston; to get there take I-93 north to exit 8 and then follow the signs. The zoo covers 26 acres and includes a large free-flight aviary. A donation of $2 for adults and $1 for children is requested.

MAPS

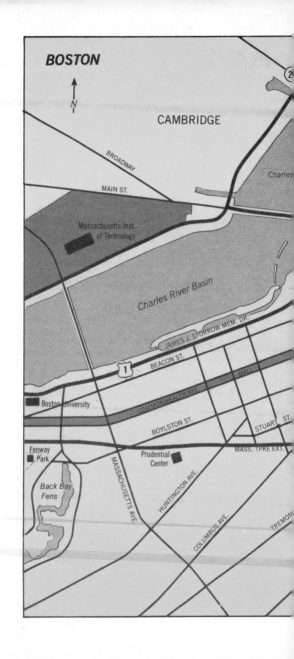

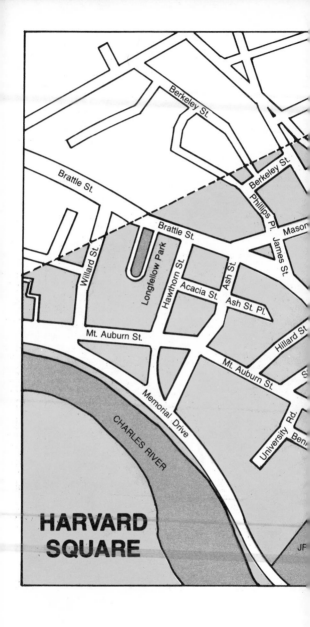

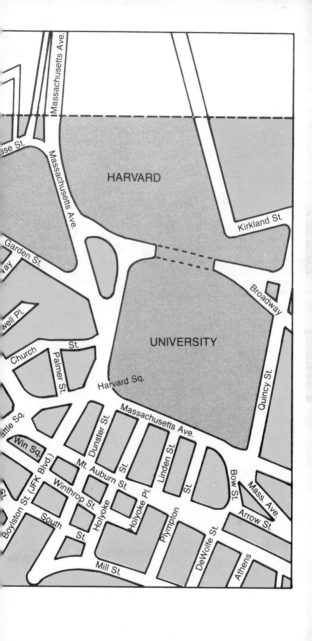

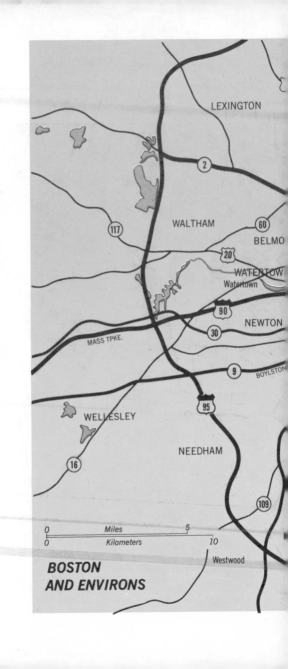

LEXINGTON

WALTHAM

BELMO

WATERTOW
Watertown

NEWTON

BOYLSTON

MASS TPKE.

WELLESLEY

NEEDHAM

Miles
0   5
0   10
Kilometers

Westwood

**BOSTON
AND ENVIRONS**

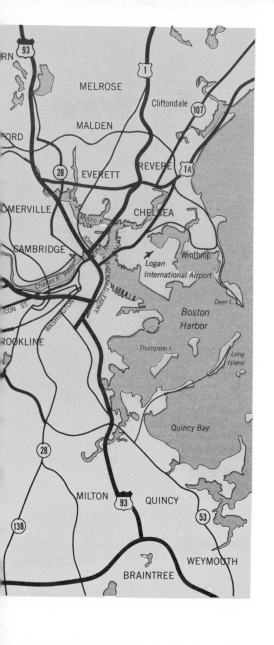

COMMUTER
RAIL
LINES

*Service to be restored—1987

Maps

CITIES IN YOUR POCKET

Barron's offers 12 fact-filled *Cities In Your Pocket* guidebooks for just $3.95 each: Atlanta (2534-2), Boston (3767-7), Chicago (3768-5), Hong Kong (3770-7), London (3760-X), Los Angeles (3759-6), New York (3755-3), Paris (3756-1), San Francisco (3758-8), Toyko (3774-X), Toronto (2836-8), and Washington, D.C. (3757-X). They're in bookstores—or order direct at address below.

LEARN A LANGUAGE

Barron's leading traveler' language aids will make your trips more satisfying. All are available in bookstores—or order direct from Barron's Educational Series, Inc., 250 Wireless Boulevard, NY 11788, and list title and number. Add 10% (1.50 minimum) for postage and handling.

French

Talking Business In French Translates 3,000 terms used in business and technology. (3745-6) $6.95

Now You're Talking French In No Time A 90-minute cassette of spoken French, 48-page audioscript and *French At A Glance* phrasebook. (7397-5) $10.95

Getting By In French A mini-course on two 60-min. cassettes with companion book. (7105-0) $16.95

Mastering French: Foreign Service Language Inst. Language Series Develops your fluency: twelve 90-min. cassettes with book. (7321-5) $75.00

German

Talking Business In German Translates 3,000 terms used in business and technology. (3747-2) $6.95

Now You're Talking German In No Time A 90-minute cassette of spoken German, 48-page audioscript and *German At A Glance* phrasebook. (7398-3) $10.95

Getting By In German A mini-course on two 60-min. cassettes with companion book. (7104-2) $16.95

Mastering German: Foreign Service Language Inst. Language Series Develops your fluency: twelve 90-min. cassettes with book. (7352-5) $75.00

Italian

Talking Business In Italian Translates 3,000 terms used in business and technology. (3754-5) $6.95

Now You're Talking Italian In No Time A 90-min. cassette of spoken Italian, 48-pg. audioscript and *Italian At A Glance* phrasebook. (7399-1) $10.95

Getting By In Italian Mini-course on two 60-min. cassettes with companion book. (7106-9) $16.95

Mastering Italian: Foreign Service Language Inst. Language Series Develops your fluency: twelve 90-min. cassettes with book. (7323-1) $75.00

Japanese

Now You're Talking Japanese In No Time 90-min. cassette of spoken Japanese, audioscript and *Japanese At A Glance* phrasebook. (7401-7) $10.95

Getting By In Japanese Mini-course on two 60-min. cassettes with companion book. (7150-6) $16.95

Spanish

Talking Business In Spanish Translates 3,000 terms used in business and technology. (3769-3) $6.95

Now You're Talking Spanish In No Time A 90-min. cassette of spoken Spanish, 4 -page audioscript and *Spanish At A Glance* phrasebook. (7400-9) $10.95

Getting By In Spanish A min-course on two 60-min. cassettes with companion book. (7103-4) $16.95

Mastering Spanish: Foreign Service Language Inst. Language Series Develops your fluency: twelve 90-min. cassettes with book. (7325-8)) $75.00